LIVING WITH A
SCENT OF
DANGER

EUROPEAN ADVENTURES AT
THE FALL OF COMMUNISM

MEMOIR
Joanne Ivy Stankievich

outskirtspress

DENVER, COLORADO

Living with a Scent of Danger
European Adventures at the Fall of Communism
All Rights Reserved.
Copyright © 2013 Joanne Ivy Stankievich
v5.0

Edited by MLG & Associates, Princeton, New Jersey
Cover Illustration by Arant Creative Group
Cover design by MLG & Associates
Back cover photo by Nancy Crabbe

Book presentations on various topics, book club activity, and interviews can be arranged through the website:
www.JoanneIvyStankievich.com

Outskirts Press, Inc.
http://www.outskirtspress.com

ISBN: 978-1-4327-7586-5

Library of Congress Control Number: 2012911099

Outskirts Press and the "OP" logo are trademarks belonging to Outskirts Press, Inc.

PRINTED IN THE UNITED STATES OF AMERICA

This book is dedicated to
my husband, Walter Stankievich,
who has been my Safe Haven for over fifty years.

TABLE OF CONTENTS

Part Two: Our World Rearranges Itself

FOREWORD

The Time Traveler and Her Husband

If you are a woman who marries an East European, you end up being married to Eastern Europe as well. If your beloved is from Belarus, you have no choice but to also enter into an intimate relationship with Belarus's mysterious history, elusive culture, fluid landscapes, soft language, and unknown future.

Which is to say: You are in for quite a ride.

The author of this book, Joanne Ivy Stankievich, found this out when she exchanged vows with Walter Stankievich, who said, "If Belarus should ever regain independence, I expect you to go with me to help rebuild my country."

Joanne was game. After all, the year was 1960, the Cold War was at its height, and any travel plans appeared more likely to be within American borders.

Eastern Europe's future was anything but certain, but in a way, it was the American hard stance against Communist totalitarianism that defined its transformation at the end of the 20th century. The "evil empire" collapsed, together with the Berlin Wall, and Eastern Europe became free. And for a beautiful, fleeting moment in history, Belarus regained independence and became a democracy.

The Congress-funded Radio Free Europe/Radio Liberty – broadcasting uncensored news behind the Iron Curtain – was in the vortex of events, both reporting on and bringing changes to Eastern Europe. That was done with the help of people like the then-Director of the Belarus Service,

Walter Stankievich, other Service Directors, and their staffs. (It was on Stankievich's invitation that I joined Radio Free Europe/Radio Liberty in 1993. In 1999, upon his retirement, I succeeded Walter as head of the Belarus Service.)

When the Soviet Union collapsed, people like Walter started to return to their native lands to become members of parliament, ambassadors, ministers, and even presidents. Time, however, flows differently in different parts of Europe, and sometimes, in opposite directions. This proved especially true in Belarus.

When Joanne and Walter started traveling across Eastern Europe, it was seemingly to travel into the past: roads, cars, hotels, food, buildings all looked frozen in time. They experienced the full spectrum of attention: they were treated as rock stars and as American spies, as dear friends and as suspicious strangers, as wise advisors and evil corrupters. For Walter, it was a part of the job description; for Joanne, it was an adventure with an uncertain end, dubious thrills, and unexpected rewards.

Unlike the time traveler in Ray Bradbury's *Sound of Thunder*, they traversed the unknown carefully and with well-earned trepidation, but over the years, Joanne and Walter helped change the future. The people who met Joanne were infected with her "can-do" enthusiasm, joyful manner, smiling radiance, and that special optimism that makes the future smile back.

This is her story. With an exacting memory and eye for details, Joanne's memoir is a spiritual and emotional journey of a woman, a couple, and a small East European country – which is to say: This book is a living history.

Her adventure may be over, but the future only begins now. Fasten your seat belts.

Alexander Lukashuk
Director, Belarus Service
Radio Free Europe/Radio Liberty
Prague, Czech Republic

(Alexander Lukashuk is a prize-winning Belarusian author of several books on Soviet history, including *Adventures of ARA in Belarus*, on the American humanitarian aid to Soviet Russia in the 1920s. His latest book, *Trace of a Butterfly, Oswald in Minsk*, published in 2012, resurrects Lee Harvey Oswald's life in Minsk in the 1960s and the travails of a troubled American defector living in Khrushchev's era.)

LIVING WITH A
SCENT OF
DANGER

Part One

THROWN INTO
INTERNATIONAL TURMOIL

EUROPEAN MAP

Displaying the previous Iron Curtain
and major cities mentioned in the book

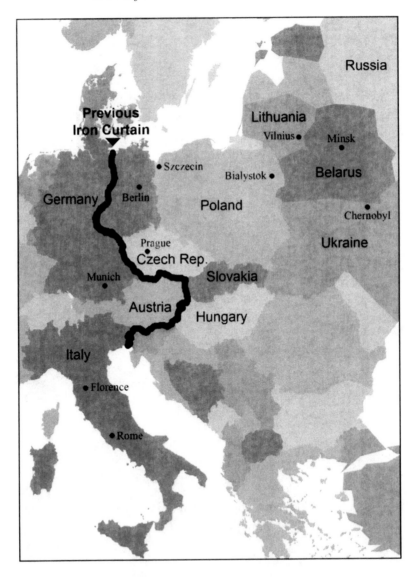

A timeline of Cold War events mentioned in the text
appears at the back of this book.

Prologue
INTO THE UNKNOWN

June 1989

Will we be safe? That was the underlying question in my mind, as I sat in our Munich apartment, thinking about the trip my husband, Walter, and I planned to take behind the infamous Iron Curtain. Admittedly, my unsettled sense was partly rooted in our recent move from the New Jersey suburbs to a cosmopolitan European city: I was still trying to navigate that wrenching shift.

The dangers inherent in this trip appeared undeniable. The Cold War was still a threatening reality. The Soviet Union dominated Eastern Europe with a sharp dividing line through the middle of Germany and Europe. Beyond those closely guarded borders were millions of people cowed by the fear that informants could, at any moment, destroy their lives. Our trip would take us into the middle of Communist society: into Czechoslovakia and Poland, through East Germany.

I tried to quiet my anxieties by reminding myself that Soviet President Gorbachev's *Glasnost* (openness) policy had brought hope of Communism loosening its grip on Eastern Europe. But as I turned on the BBC TV news that evening, images of heavily armed policemen attacking peaceful Solidarity demonstrators in Poland underscored the continuing dangers.

A complicating factor: Walter worked at the Belarus Service of Radio Free Europe/Radio Liberty (commonly referred to as the Radios or RFE/RL). I knew those broadcasts had been continuously jammed by the Soviets, but I hadn't thought much about any possible danger related to Walter's work, until my first visit to the Munich headquarters last fall. There, I learned that several Radios colleagues had been murdered, presumably by Soviet agents.

The main reason for our trip was to visit Walter's relatives in Czechoslovakia and Poland. Walter was born in the then-Polish city of Wilno (Vilnia in Belarusian, now called Vilnius, as the capital of Lithuania), but his family identified closely with their Belarusian heritage. Because Walter's father, Jan Stankievich, worked actively for Belarusian independence, he fled the on-coming Soviets at the start of World War II. Walter's mother (Mary Novak Stankievich) then took Walter and his two brothers to live in relative safety with her family in Prague. Walter had strong memories of his nurturing Czech relatives. Consequently, with the more liberated atmosphere that Glasnost promised, he wanted to risk visiting them.

Most of my information on Eastern Europe came from the news and spy stories. However, International Relations had been my minor at college, so I'd been following the Cold War closely for some time. The idea of going behind the Iron Curtain – to see how valid my impressions were – intrigued and fascinated me, even while it created apprehension over our safety.

That evening, we sat in our quiet reading mode after dinner: I, with a le Carre novel in hand; Walter, with reams of daily news reports to digest. It was a furnished apartment provided by the Radios, but made to feel like home with decorations of our own, including an Austrian wood sculpture of a poacher and a minimalistic Chinese painting of vegetables.

My thoughts were distracted from the novel, for I needed to get my concerns in the open before we actually finalized plans. So I broached the question,

"Walter, I was just thinking about the trip, and wondering whether we might have any problems with the Soviets, because of your family history. Do you think they'll be aware of us – that we might be followed or harassed in some way?" He laid his papers down on the coffee table, as he looked up with a frown on his round

Slavic face.

"Oh come on, Joanne, you read too many spy stories. The Radios approved our trip. I don't think they'd have done that, if they felt we'd be in danger."

"I guess things *are* getting better now, with Glasnost and all," I replied.

"This trip is important to me," he asserted. "I haven't seen my Prague relatives since we left in such a hurry in '45 (when the Soviet troops entered the city). Cousin Mirek said Aunt Anichka is ill. I feel like we need to go there now, while we have the chance." He was thoughtful for a minute, then added, "You know, we can't be sure how long this openness will last. It could be short-lived, like the '68 Prague Spring."

That struck a nerve with me, but I kept quiet. The truth was that a hard-line Soviet crackdown could happen at any time. And I didn't want to be in Eastern Europe if it did.

On the other hand, I didn't really want to give in to my fears, either. I upbraided myself: Joanne, you need to stop this nonsense. You're letting your fears and imagination rule you. Walter's probably right; the Soviets may not even notice us traveling through. So just go on the trip and enjoy it – and leave your safety in Higher hands.

I'd made my decision. It was time to move forward.

"I certainly understand you wanting to visit family while we're in Europe. Okay then, let's get this itinerary planned out." I picked up maps of Germany, Poland, and Czechoslovakia and started marking them, since I was going to be the main navigator on the trip. It would be my responsibility to make sure no wrong turn inadvertently took us where foreigners weren't allowed. Recently, a tourist had been jailed for that same mistake.

As we talked about the Prague part of the trip, Walter cautioned me,

"Now remember, if anyone asks, we're just visiting my ailing aunt Anichka. It might cause the others difficulties, if it's known we're seeing them as well."

Walter must have noted the concern in my eyes. He came over, fluffed my short white hair, put a reassuring arm around me, and said, "We'll be fine." I leaned into his quiet strength and some of my tenseness began to dissipate.

When Walter ambled off to his study, I hunkered down in the deep, brown velour sofa in the living room. I thought back to my sheltered childhood on a small farm in Washington State. I remembered myself as a pre-teen, daydreaming, as I swung back and forth on an old tire that was tied to the cherry tree in the back yard. My aspiration was to someday live in sophisticated New York City, maybe even travel to ancient cities in Europe, and have exciting adventures. However, until I was 18, I'd never traveled more than 100 miles from that farm and small hometown.

This life in Europe seemed like a culmination of my childhood dreams. But, now that the trip into what might be "enemy territory" was almost upon us, my thoughts kept shifting between anxiety and anticipation.

My mind flashed back to how this European adventure had started a year and a half earlier ...

Our suburban home in Mountain Lakes, New Jersey

1
JOB LOSS: DISASTER OR OPPORTUNITY?

Mountain Lakes, New Jersey, December 1987

It was a warm Monday morning, not typical for a winter's day. Hunched over my office desk, I was writing up an order for our part-time marketing business when the phone rang. I straightened, put my pen down, and answered with a cheery "Hello."

"Joanne…" It was my husband's voice – which was unexpected, because he rarely called me from his engineering job in Paramus. I wondered what was wrong.

"I don't have good news," Walter continued. "Remember last week when the company asked me to fly home early from California?"

"Yeah, it seemed strange. Were they unhappy that you stayed over the weekend to finish the job?"

"It was pretty ironic, really. I was being so responsible to stay and finish the job right for them, and you know what? They only wanted me back Thursday so they could fire me on Friday."

I let out a subdued "Oh," and let him finish. "Our whole group was laid off Friday, including my boss." It wasn't a total surprise. Walter had told me that the company didn't get the new contract it had bid on.

I remained quiet for a moment, trying to quell my rising concerns. In our business, we'd been training associates to embrace the positive side of any situation. "Challenges are really just opportunities," we'd remind them. Although I sometimes react to small annoyances, when there's a big challenge I usually adhere to the positive-response dictum.

So I said, "Okay, this is just an opportunity, and that's the only way we're going to look at it."

"That's the right attitude," Walter agreed. "I'll be home early, maybe around three. We can talk more about it then. I just thought I ought to let you know what's happened."

I replaced the phone and sat there thinking. Recently, we'd put an addition onto our house so that Walter's ailing mother could live with us. Sadly, she was gone now, but we were still paying off bills for the addition. Our older son, John, had graduated, but we still had several more years of college tuition ahead of us for our younger son, Steve. And just months before, I'd stressed our financial situation even more by accompanying some business associates to Italy, expanding our marketing activities there. My conclusion: we really couldn't afford Walter being unemployed, even for a short time.

I set aside my work, no longer the most important task of the day. Being a life-long person of faith, I was used to turning to God for answers to all my needs – whether for guidance, protection, or healing. So I grabbed a heavy sweater, took my Bible, and headed for the sunny back deck. Removed from the busy Boulevard, our contemporary Mountain Lakes home was on a secluded wooded lot. I sat there quietly for a few minutes, gazing out onto the woods. I spied a red cardinal in the evergreen tree; a blue jay cawed loudly. I felt the serenity of being at-one with nature, and my thoughts began to lift beyond the questions in my mind.

I read some reassuring lines from the 23rd Psalm: "The Lord is my shepherd; I shall not want. He maketh me to lie down in green pastures: he leadeth me beside the still waters . . . Surely goodness and mercy shall follow me all the days of my life." From this, I felt assured that, whatever happened, God would support and direct our decisions, and the outcome would be good.

Around noon the next day, Walter came into the kitchen wearing his comfortable chinos, instead of his suit and tie. He was beaming a smile at me, but I noticed his eyes held concern.

"I've been calling around," he said. "Some of my regular contacts are now unemployed in this downturn, too. You know, I'm 55 and not totally up-to-date on new engineering technology. It may not be so easy to get a job this time."

"Well, if things aren't so good around here, then let's not limit ourselves to just this area. We've been in Mountain Lakes for almost 20 years. The kids are in college. It might be interesting to move somewhere else." I was confident we'd be okay. In the past, Walter had changed jobs at the end of contracts, and he'd always quickly gotten another job, usually a better position with a higher salary.

Several weeks went by, and Walter still didn't have a job offer. He seemed quieter than usual, obviously worried about our situation. I was beginning to see that this might be a longer process than other times. Gradually, we opened our minds to other possibilities.

A conversation we had long ago kept nagging at the back of my mind. One evening, as we sat cozily in front of the fireplace, I decided to broach the topic.

"Hon, let's think out-of-the-box for a minute about your work. We do that with others, maybe it's time to do it for ourselves." Walter agreed.

"What do you have in mind?"

"Well, remember when you said that engineering hadn't been your first love and that history was your favorite subject in college?"

"But what can I do with that? ... Actually, several years ago, a friend in broadcasting suggested my going to Munich to work at the Belarus Service of Radio Free Europe/Radio Liberty."

"Yeah, I recall that. It wasn't a good time for us then, with the kids in high school, but maybe we're in a better position to do it now. In fact, this could be a very interesting time to go to Europe, given Gorbachev's Glasnost policies."

"You're right. I wonder if they still need someone in the Belarus Service. I'll work on my resume and send it off." I saw a glimmer of excitement spread across Walter's face. It made me feel as if we were headed in the right direction.

Walter had always been involved in Belarusian activities: he participated in the Brooklyn-based Belarus Dance Group; helped to establish Belair Miensk, a Belarusian resort in the Catskills; and he'd also served as President of the Belarusian-American Association. I knew how important his national identity was to him, and I wanted to continue supporting those activities. If Walter goes to work at the Radios, I thought, it will give him an opportunity to contribute something even more significant to his country of origin.

Fortunately, the Radios were interested in Walter's Belarusian connections, and they called him for an interview at their headquarters in Washington, D.C. (although most of the operation was in Munich). After the interview, they indicated that they wanted to employ him, but said they had no current openings in either research or broadcasting at that time. They wound up offering him a position as Program Reviewer. Walter pondered what to do. It wasn't a job he'd want on a long-term basis, but at least he'd be on location, and it would probably be easier to transfer to a desired position later. He accepted the offer.

I'm sure Walter had qualms about whether the new job would work out. He had occasionally written articles for Belarusian publications in the States. However, since he didn't have any formal training in journalism, he immediately enrolled in a New York University course on investigative reporting.

I felt proud of my husband. He was courageous enough to start a new career at 55 and make such a dramatic shift: from engineering to journalism.

I also felt great relief. I hoped his accepting the position meant our financial worries were over. Unfortunately, my relief was short-lived. We hadn't realized how many more months we'd have to wait for the completion of the background security checks, before Walter could actually start working.

Family: Walter, Joanne, girlfriend Heather with Steve, John

2
LEAVING OUR COMFORT ZONE

It ended up being nine months of unemployment before Walter's steady income resumed. Although it was a financially strapped period, we needed all that time to prepare for the move, which included: rearranging our business activity; selling our house and furnishings; and making different living arrangements for our sons, John and Steve. I wondered how they would handle these drastic changes to their lives and how our move might impact our relationship with them. They had been the center of our lives for the last 20 years.

Earlier, during the fall of 1987, the boys had gone on an adventure to Colorado with some friends. More recently, they'd run out of money and returned home. One night, Walter and I asked them to stick around after dinner because we had something important to discuss.

The boys, sprawled out on our sectional white sofas, waited impatiently to hear what we had to say. Walter quickly got their attention, as he told them our decision to move to Europe and sell our Mountain Lakes house.

"What?" I can still see the shock on Steve's round face. (He has that same Stankievich, Slavic look as his father.) Obviously, he was having a hard time comprehending our plan. Not only were we going to leave Mountain Lakes, but also move 3,000 miles to a different continent. Steve was the more family-oriented of the two boys, so I recognized our leaving might affect him more than John.

"You're selling our house?" John said. "But that's where we get together with all our friends. What are we going to do?" John was the more independent and strong-willed son, but he did consider our Mountain Lakes home his party house. Obviously, too, the boys viewed our home as a secure place they could always come back to, as they'd recently done.

"Hey, it's been a great house and town to grow up in," I answered, "but you're both going off in new directions now. You can always visit your friends at their houses." They didn't look comforted with that idea, but Walter went on to share another part of our plan.

"John, it looks like you'll need some more practical training to get a good job. We could fund you taking a course on computer technology at Chubb Institute, if that would help." John's thin frame stretched out, in a more relaxed way, and he nodded in approval. Still, all he said was a quiet "Uh huh." He'd been delivering pizzas for extra cash, and we knew it was disappointing to him that he hadn't gotten a permanent job yet.

"Steve, since you're planning on going back to Rutgers in the fall, maybe you and John can rent a house in the New Brunswick area to share with other students." Also, Walter and I would feel better knowing they'd be together for support.

Walter tried to reassure them, "We'll come back for some of the holidays, and you can visit us in Europe."

After our discussion with the boys, I vacillated between feeling guilty about leaving them and justifying our actions. I could see how they might feel somewhat abandoned by us, and that made me regretful. On the other hand, I reminded myself that John was 24 and Steve 20. We'd focused on giving them the best we could when they were growing up, and now it was time for all of us to move on with our lives.

And, I suppose typically for someone who'd grown up during the Great Depression, I couldn't feel too sorry for them. My childhood had been confined to our farm and the small town of Monroe, Washington, without any vacations. Then, when I was 13, my father (Dan Ivy) died in a farm accident, and our lives changed for the worse. There wasn't much insurance and little income, so my mother (Esther Hulseman Dean Ivy) – who'd had her own secretarial agency in Seattle – took a job as a cook in the kitchen of our high school, so that she could return home from work at the same time as school ended. My mom; my younger sister, Jewell; and I had to move from the big farmhouse to a smaller house on the property, which didn't have running water or indoor plumbing. Years later, a classmate commented on how changed I was after my father's death: from a carefree, laughing teen to a very serious one.

Walter's childhood during World War II included memories of his hiding when German bombs exploded over Vilnia; an arduous trek through war-ravaged Poland to relatives in Prague; and, at the end of the war, the ominous KGB knock on the door that propelled the family into four years in Displaced Persons camps, before coming to the United States.

In contrast, I felt that our children had had a good life. We'd moved to Mountain Lakes to give our boys the best school system we could find in northern New Jersey. It was an upscale community, and Walter and I had to work hard in our part-time business to afford living there. But we never regretted the excellent education and good life that the boys experienced, and we enjoyed participating in the community as well.

We also traveled with them cross-country in a motor home several times to Mexico and the Pacific Northwest, and we snorkeled together in the Caribbean. Both boys had enjoyed trips to Europe before college. Besides, independence was a quality instilled in me by my pioneering father and passed on to the boys; I thought that would benefit them when on their own.

My concern about the boys was also assuaged in part because, during their childhoods, I'd looked to God as their ultimate parent, additionally providing for their fathering and mothering needs in myriad ways, beyond our parenting. It was therefore natural for me to feel prayerfully confident that the boys would be provided with a comforting sense of home, wherever they were.

It did cross my mind, fleetingly, that maybe my defensiveness masked guilt – I just wasn't going to dwell on it. It's my motto: once a decision is made, just move forward and don't look back.

During this preparation time, discouragement sometimes tried to overwhelm me. Five months after listing the house with a realtor, I wailed,

"Walter, what are we going to do? We need the money from the sale of the house to pay off these bills."

"We'll just have to do the best we can," was all Walter could answer. During the previous year, homes in Mountain Lakes had often sold over the asking price. Unfortunately, the month before we listed the house, mortgage rates suddenly rose, and the real estate market plummeted.

Naturally, I prayed about the situation. Sometimes money came from unexpected sources, just when we needed it. But, for a couple of important bills, we felt embarrassed for having to delay payment – we'd never done that before. Eventually, the house was rented, but it was almost two years before it finally sold.

Those months were a busy, chaotic time, often filled with tension and uncertainty. Sometimes the calming influence was Walter, giving me a hug or gentle response like, "Now Joanne, it's going to be alright." Other times, I'd disappear into the bedroom to play tapes of soothing hymns, and listen to them over and over, until my thoughts were lifted up. Then, I'd share an idea with Walter that had inspired me.

We tried different approaches to handling our situation. We'd taught goal setting, visualization, and positive affirmations in our business, so we placed cards with present-positive statements around the house, such as, "I feel confident in my new job with RFE/RL." After some research, I visualized which area of Munich I'd like to live in and then added a card: "Our beautiful new home in Bogenhausen has a relaxing, homey atmosphere."

We'd been told that the Radios provided all the furnishings in their allotted apartments in Munich. Consequently, we sold most of our furniture, stored a few keepsakes, and packed only clothing and some favorite decorative pieces for shipment to Europe. This left us with bare necessities for a couple of weeks before departure, but it pinpointed something for me. Hey, I thought, this is really liberating: to divest ourselves of all these accumulated material possessions. Now we can go wherever inspiration leads us and focus on "doing" rather than "getting."

Toward the end of this period, I looked back and thought, It's true, trials often make us stronger. I could see that I'd learned to let go of some of my more controlling nature and instead trust that all would be well. Often, when starting to feel overwhelmed, I'd remind myself that – after all this turmoil was finished – we would be heading into an expansive new adventure.

An increasing worry welled up in me, however, as I turned my thoughts toward our new life in Munich. We would be leaving behind much of what had defined us for so long: being Mountain Lakers, parenting our two sons, and creating a successful business. Walter was a respected engineer and Belarusian activist; I was a member of the League of Women Voters, the American Association of University Women, on the Mountain Lakes Environmental Commission, and active in my church.

In Munich, Walter had a defined role waiting for him, but I was going to be starting over with a blank slate. I presumed we'd have some interesting trips around Europe, and I certainly would be supporting Walter in his new venture. On the other hand, I didn't want to be just an adjunct to my husband. I questioned how I would redefine myself in this new environment. What kind of worthwhile activity could I find? Where would I find meaningful relationships?

Living in Europe wasn't going to be a totally new experience, however. We'd lived in Europe before, in the early 1960s, when Walter had an engineering job installing communications systems for NATO, but it was a different experience than what I expected this time. Then, we moved every three months, so we never put down roots anywhere. Also, our first son, John, was born just two months after arrival, so our focus during those three years was on him. Our activities outside the home were mainly skiing and tourism, and most of our associations were with co-workers. My hope was that, this time, we could become more a part of the local culture.

Finally, in August of 1988, Walter received the last of the high security clearances needed for his new job. By the time we boarded the plane to Germany in early September, we were exhausted, physically and emotionally. Settling into our seats, I whispered to Walter, "This is really going to be an exciting adventure!" I snuggled close to him and put my head on his shoulder. We held hands most of the rest of that sleepless night – trying to reassure each other, as we flew toward an uncertain future.

Decorated Bavarian house

3
CHALLENGES IN MUNICH

On the plane, I kept conjuring up what our life might be like in Munich.

Munich! The very name evoked certain stereotypes: of carousing Oktoberfest Bavarians wearing lederhosen and of Nazis saluting Hitler in the Munich Hofbrauhaus. I remembered hearing Frankfurters – back when we lived in Europe in the '60s – scoff at Bavarians as being farmers with a local accent. I was eager to have those images revised with facts.

My enthusiasm for our new Munich experience bubbled over, even before the plane set down. As the plane descended, I could see tractor cuts curving around what appeared to be undulating hills, outside the city of Munich. Then farmhouses and herds of milk cows became visible. At the center of each small village I saw a church with a high steeple. My farm memories resonated with the scene, though these farms looked much tidier than our 25 acres back in Monroe, where rusted-out pick-ups were often hidden behind the dilapidated woodshed.

As we disembarked, my creeping anxiety was quieted when I spied someone holding a Radio Free Europe/Radio Liberty sign. Our assigned host, Liz, helped us load our luggage into the Radios van, and we drove through the countryside toward Munich, getting a close-up view of the Bavarian farms and villages that I'd seen from the plane. Many of the village houses had exposed dark wood cross-beams, and their outer walls were covered with paintings: of horse-drawn wagons, or festival scenes with musicians and costumed revelers. Also catching my attention were the carved wooden balconies with their boxes of cascading red geraniums.

Besides the orderliness of the farms, I saw other indications of what I'd considered a German trait of fastidiousness. As we drove through a forest, the sides of the road appeared almost manicured. Then, passing through a small town, I noticed several women sweeping the sidewalk in front of their homes. As we came into the city, the streets seemed much cleaner than any New Jersey city. So far, I was impressed with our new environment.

Liz took us to our assigned apartment on Siegfriedstrasse in Schwabing, a thriving artists' section of Munich. I felt comforted when she commented that the building was leased exclusively by the Radios. Good, I thought, I can make friends right here.

My initial enthusiasm quickly turned to disappointment, however, when Liz pointed out our apartment building. On the outside of the old, tenement-like building was a scrawl of hateful graffiti objecting to *Auslaenders* (foreigners) in the neighborhood. How could I invite new friends to a home with such ugly words greeting them?

We walked around the apartment with Liz to get a sense of the layout. I wanted to focus on any good interior features, rather than the exterior. Fortunately, the high ceilings and large windows appealed to me. The two-bedroom apartment had just been repainted and refurbished, so at least it was fresh and clean.

"You're lucky," Liz said. "Others still have old, mismatched furniture from the Radios' early days." The curved, blond furniture was very different from the straight-lined, dark walnut look that had been our choice in America. But the light color helped to make the cozy living-dining room appear larger (and it was certainly better than having mismatched furniture).

After Walter and I signed the necessary papers, Liz departed, and I inspected the apartment more carefully. I made a discovery: there was only a mini-sized refrigerator in the kitchen.

"Walter, come and look at this tiny refrigerator," I yelled across the apartment. "Do you think we could ask for a larger one?" He was reorganizing the extra bedroom to use as his office and wasn't overly concerned about the size of the refrigerator at that moment.

"No, I'm not even going to ask," Walter responded. "That's the kind of refrigerator people have in Europe. You'll just have to get used to it." His voice had an uncharacteristically sharp edge (usually he's soft-spoken and kind). I guessed he didn't want to request special favors, being the new American colleague among the mostly European personnel at the Radios.

But I was tired and piqued by his answer. "Well, you could at least try," I grumbled under my breath. I didn't want to spend time every day shopping for food. Maybe we'll eat out more, I decided.

As the days passed, challenges confronted me every day, and I struggled to adjust.

For example, my first day introduced me to a new way of

shopping. As I picked up a few basic items at the nearest store, I observed how the locals shopped: many had personal metal shopping carts that they wheeled from store to store. The next morning, I purchased a cart at Hertie's, a nearby department store, and then started my trek up and down the crowded nearby shopping streets. Each store specialized in just one type of food – and many foods were very different from those I was used to buying in an American supermarket.

I was delighted by the variety of breads at the bakery, where I chose the *Sonnenblumenbrot* (dark bread with sunflower seeds). Also enticing was the dessert window in the *Konditorei* (candy and pastry shop), with its display of marzipan candies in animal forms. For dessert, I chose a luscious-looking dark chocolate cake called *Sacher torte*. Admittedly, I'm a bit of a chocoholic.

I had to learn some lessons: a disapproving finger wagged at me when I tried to reach for oranges at the fruit stand, self-service evidently being a cultural taboo.

At the meat market, another problem presented itself. I wanted hamburger, so I looked up the word for "ground" meat in my ever-present dictionary. When it was my turn at the counter, I said *"Bodenfleisch, bitte."* The man behind the counter frowned; he seemed angry with me. Unfortunately, the translation sounded to him as if I wanted meat from off the floor (ground). After several minutes of confusion, an English-speaking customer asked me what I really wanted and then explained to the merchant that I wanted *Hackfleisch* (minced meat). I wrote the word down for future reference; otherwise, we'd never be able to have good old American hamburger again.

That shopping experience left me exhausted and wondering how I was going to do that every few days.

Most of my communication attempts in the early days revolved around shopping. I did learn some tricks to assist me. For instance, when asking for an item in a store, if I asked in English, "Do you speak English?" almost invariably the answer was "Nein," with the saleslady turning her back to me. But if I asked her the same question in my very bad German, she'd often recognize that her English was better than my German, and she'd answer, "Yes, a little." And we'd be on our way to a sale.

I knew that learning German was important, so that first week I signed up for private lessons at the Berlitz School. Remembering the German words wasn't a problem, but when I pronounced them, the teacher grimaced. I obviously didn't have an ear for reproducing the sounds. (I also can't carry a tune, which may be related.)

I worried about the long-term implications of this inability to learn languages. How will I be able to acclimate to my new environment, if I can't communicate clearly with others? What if I want to continue our business in Europe? How could I do that, speaking only English? Also, I had been presuming that Walter would want to go back to America when his job was over. But, being European, what if he decided he was more comfortable staying here? That last idea frightened me, so I decided to think only about the present moment.

My introduction to a new culture was sometimes disconcerting. On the first Sunday after moving to Schwabing, we donned comfortable clothes to stroll along paths in the nearby *Englischer Garten*. This large park had meadows, lovely wooded areas, and a stream running down to the Isar River. The sound of music in the distance attracted us toward the *Chinesische Turm* (Chinese Tower). The Turm was a tall, open tower, with a surrounding outdoor *Biergarten*, which had long, wooden communal tables and chairs. Walter explained that the occasional pots we saw hung on posts were "honey pots" – placed there to attract the buzzing wasps away from the beer.

Local people welcomed strangers at their tables with jovial good humor, as their quart-sized beer mugs clanged together vigorously. In the center of the Biergarten was a small wooden platform, whereupon dancers in lederhosen clapped their hands, leapt into the air, and slapped their thighs to the music of a three-piece brass band. It seemed a stereotypical scene, yet just the lively Bavarian atmosphere I'd been seeking.

We skirted the lake (the *Kleinhesseloher See*) and stood awhile, watching people in small paddle-boats. Such a calming contrast to the bustling city life just blocks away! This is almost like New York City's Central Park, I thought – except, unlike in Central Park, most people appeared to be dressed in their Sunday best.

Then suddenly, as we walked around a bend in the stream, we came upon a group of people with a noticeably different idea of a Sunday outing.

"Oh my gosh," I said, as I averted my eyes. A man was standing up, stretching nonchalantly, and he was completely nude. In fact, the whole group was lolling around naked.

"How can they allow that, right where families with young children are walking?" I whispered to Walter.

"No one else seems to be perturbed by it," he answered, gesturing around at the other strollers. I looked around and saw that he was right; no one seemed the least bit concerned.

I recalled hearing that, until recently, infidelity during *Fasching* (Germany's Mardi Gras) could not be used as grounds for divorce, since it was quite acceptable. These mores were very different from the ones I'd been taught to follow.

My somewhat conservative radar was now on the alert. A week

later, as our bus drove by a nearby industrial section, I pointed to some houses, and asked Walter,

"Is that what I think it is?" There were red lights in the windows of the houses and signs decorated with scantily-clad women.

"Probably," Walter replied. "They look like government-approved houses of prostitution. I guess they're here for the truckers in this area." I was surprised at Walter's answer, but then I recalled seeing a number of men walking around Schwabing in women's attire, and I understood why a friend referred to our area as Sodom and Gomorrah. From her standpoint, all of these activities must have seemed similar to those in Biblical times.

It did appear that there was a different attitude about morals in Europe. I wondered, Are these customs prevalent in Germany only, or in other European countries as well? I considered a potential dilemma: as we become more immersed in the local culture, how can I remain non-judgmental, while not subscribing to these different standards myself?

By the end of September, I was feeling isolated, having spent most of my days – and even evenings – alone in a foreign country. Walter was immersed in his work at Broadcast Analysis, where he critiqued the Radios' programming for factual accuracy and avoidance of excessive nationalism. Every evening, he brought home reams of news analysis to study, so that he could keep updated on world events.

One day, I saw a poster for Oktoberfest, which was being held at the *Theresienwiese* fairgrounds, so after dinner, I said,

"Walter, I might not come from the States for Oktoberfest, but since we're already here, how about going?"

I was surprised when he answered, "That sounds like fun. I'm ready for a break." Me too, I thought.

We went on Saturday evening. As we came out of the crowded U-Bahn subway car, we joined a crush of people moving toward the fairgrounds entrance gate. Music was blasting from several huge tents, each one holding thousands of people. Walter explained that each tent represented a different local brewery.

Entering one tent, I was visually accosted by wobbling, big-bellied, leder-hosened men getting up on long tables to perform. They were holding their quart-sized mugs of beer in one hand, while waving the other to the deafening oompah music. Some stomped their feet, most of them were shouting, and all swayed as one body to the music: "Ole, Ole, Ole!"

Some Oktoberfest visitors got further into the mood by grabbing strangers to dance in the narrow aisles, hindering the flow of food to tables. The waitresses wore aprons over fully-petticoated skirts. Their embroidered blouses were tightly fitted, exposing deep cleavage, which – observing the drunken leers and pats on the rear – seemed to be gratefully appreciated by the male customers. The wild atmosphere in the tent was fun at first, but soon the incredible din of loud music and shouting became too much for me, and I opted to leave for the quieter outside crowds.

As we left, I glimpsed a brightly lit up amusement park section, with a Ferris wheel and other rides, toward the back of the tent area. Along the sides, there were stalls selling heart-shaped cookies and trinkets and small *Imbiss* (snack) counters with pretzels and sausages. We had to jump out of the way as a bedecked team of horses barreled along with a cart full of beer kegs to replenish the Oktoberfest thirst.

"Hey, look at those fish all lined up on long sticks over hot coals. What is that?" I asked Walter.

He read from the sign: "'Vromfischer' is the name of the tent, and 'Steckerlfisch' indicates how they are being cooked – on a stick."

I wanted to know what kind of fish they were, and Walter explained that they had several kinds, but suggested our trying the grilled mackerel.

We stood in a long line for the fish, but it was worth it. In contrast to my memory of tough mackeral, this was tender and moist inside the crispy, salted skin, and it was served simply, in a piece of foil. Each bite pulled away easily with the small wooden fork they provided. Walter had a beer with it, but I bought a hot pretzel to offset the fish taste and capped it off with a refreshing mug of *Apfelschorle* (a combination of apple juice and sparkling water).

Later, we stopped at the Krems booth to order some of their baseball-sized *Dampfnudel* (dumplings), served with vanilla sauce, cinnamon, sugar, and poppy seeds on top; the combination melted smoothly in my mouth. I'd found my reason to return to Oktoberfest another year: for the special foods, not the beer tents.

Although Oktoberfest seemed unique, there was also a very different Bavarian – and not just German – flavor to where we lived. There was the bawdy humor; the beer hall *stammtisches* (regular tables), where friends met weekly; and the "Oompah" bands in the parks and outdoor restaurants. What I'd thought of as costumes (called *Tracht*) exclusively worn at Oktoberfest were also considered proper Sunday attire in Munich – and were even worn as everyday clothing in Bavarian villages. Bavaria definitely offered a very different way of life compared to Frankfurt, the austere financial center where we'd lived in the 1960s. I liked Munich's more farmer-oriented and colorful atmosphere, although I was still having trouble adjusting to it.

RFE/RL postcard of Mir castle in Belarus

4

POTENTIAL DANGERS LOOM

The next week I had to go to the Radio Free Europe/Radio Liberty headquarters to fill out some legal papers, allowing me to stay in the country.

The headquarters was a forbidding sight. First, there was a high wall topped with barbed wire; while inside the gate, armed guards patrolled the grounds. The sentinel at the front gate called Walter to vouch for me and escort me inside. At the main entrance, I had to stop again for additional ID checks and then was told to leave my bag at the check-in counter.

"What's with all this security? Isn't Munich a safe enough city?" I questioned.

"In 1981, a bomb was set off at the side of the building, severely damaging it and injuring some members of the Czech

Service. That's when they put all this up," Walter responded.

"Who did that?"

"I was told it was the work of the terrorist, Carlos the Jackal, contracted by the Romanian Intelligence Service – I'm sure, with Soviet encouragement."

"Really?" I was dumbfounded. I'd read about Carlos in news articles and spy novels. It was alarming to think that I was standing where he'd actually operated. I also felt unsettled by the thought that the headquarters in Munich, where Walter worked, might still be a target of the Soviets.

Walter took me on a tour of the Radios building. The offices of the Ukrainian Service were in one wing, the Belarusian offices in another; with offices for the string of Soviet-controlled countries continuing on down the corridor. Interspersed throughout the building were acoustically-sealed studios, each equipped for on-going short-wave radio programming. Several people dashed past us down the hallway, with the latest news ready for broadcasting. I was impressed by the extensiveness of the Radios operation and felt proud of my husband's participation in this effort to offset Communism's media control.

We decided to have lunch in the basement cafeteria with other Belarus Service staff – about ten, at that time. I noticed that different languages were spoken at the lunch tables. The Belarusian spoken at our table halted as we approached; then Walter introduced me. The group started reminiscing in English about some of the events during their time at the Radios. As they talked, my concerns grew.

"We have to be careful, 'they' (I presumed they meant Soviet provocateurs) had a plan to put poison in the salt shakers one time," said one staff member. Looking at the salt, pepper, and sugar containers on the table, I decided I didn't need to add anything to my food.

"Remember when poor Lavon (Leanid Karas) didn't show up for work at our Service and later was found floating in the Isar River?"

"Oh yes, and how cautious we all got the year (Georgi) Markov was killed in London with a poisoned umbrella tip?"

"And then Stepan Bandera, the former Ukrainian Partisan Army leader, was murdered, right in his Munich apartment."

I wanted to yell "Stop!" Were they trying to impress me with the danger of their work? I was shaking when I left that encounter.

The conversation had a lasting effect: for three weeks I had a recurring dream of men bursting into our apartment with machine guns. Each night, for months, I carefully checked the locks on our apartment door at bedtime.

That visit made me wonder if *we* might also encounter dangers associated with Radios work, during our own stay. I reasoned that I couldn't do anything to change the situation of the Soviets wanting to shut down the Radios. So I made a conscious decision to simply not carry those concerns as a constant fear and to focus on trusting God to protect us. But, I'll admit, it took me some time and many prayers before I felt secure again.

Within two weeks, we were invited to our first social event with other Belarusians. The party was meant to welcome us to the Service and was held at the apartment of Larysa, one of the Service members. Most of the Service personnel were invited, as well as some other Belarusians who'd settled in Munich because of the nucleus of the Service community.

Before leaving for the party, I checked myself in the mirror. Our extended wardrobe (with party clothes) hadn't arrived yet by ship, but I felt my mahogany soft-suede suit looked quite dressy, contrasting with my white hair, which was highlighted by the pearls around my neck. I wanted to make a good first impression with these Belarusians who would be a vital part of Walter's life and work in Munich.

I glanced over at Walter, who looked distinguished in his jade suit, soft-yellow shirt, and green and gold striped tie. It perfectly accented his blond hair and golden brown eyes. But then, I'm prejudiced: I've always felt that those gentle eyes – with the crinkle at the corners when he smiles – are one of his best features.

Disembarking from the *Strassenbahn* rail line, and approaching Larysa's apartment building, I stopped for a minute to check my lipstick and hair.

At the door, Larysa greeted us warmly,

"*Dobry dzien* (good day), *Viachka* (Walter's shortened Belarusian name). We're so glad you could come, Joanne." I noted that she was wearing a fancy blue taffeta dress and dramatic earrings that set off her long dark hair. It made me wish our party clothes had arrived.

Larysa ushered us into a noisy room full of people. Walter shook hands with the men, and hugged some of the women, introducing me along the way. Several men stood, bowed, and kissed my hand, in true European style. I could see that a couple of the women were sizing up "Viachka's American wife," as they looked at me sideways and commented to others.

As I watched my husband, I thought, It's good to see Walter animatedly talking politics with compatriots. In American groups he was often very quiet.

I walked around the room, looking at the decor. It was quite different from my minimalistic taste: large, dark, carved furniture and colorful Persian rugs filled the room. And there was much artwork; along with a few Belarusian paintings, there were masks and artifacts from South Africa, where Larysa often visited a friend.

Helena spoke more English than some of the others and tried to make me feel comfortable by chatting in English. Then I helped set the table, noting the strong garlic fragrance of the kielbasa wafting in the air.

After the meal, the vodka drinking started. One of Walter's attractive characteristics is his moderation. He knows I don't drink, and usually he drinks only one beer or a glass of wine when we go out. His way of handling this kind of situation – common at Belarusian parties – was to barely sip from the shot glass, thus never needing a refill.

As the bottle came around a third time, I edged close to Walter and whispered,

"Walter, I don't think you need any more." But my admonition was caught by the Director, rumored to be a heavy drinker.

"Aaah," he slurred, leaning closer, "Valter, you're not going to let your wife tell you what to do, are you?" He was challenging both of us. I guess Walter noted my set jaw and defiant eyes, because he quickly intervened.

"Joanne, it's okay, we're just enjoying an evening together." Walter fluffed me off, with a "Be Quiet" hand motion.

"See, good-ole Valter isn't going to be hen-pecked by a wife."

I was insulted and felt humiliated that my husband was not standing up for me. I didn't like what was going on.

Finally I rose, saying, "Walter, I'm really tired, we need to get going." We said our good-byes and left.

I was up several times that night – crying, praying, and trying to think through how to approach Walter about the evening's events. It wasn't just the drinking that night that bothered me. I worried if, in this new environment, increased drinking might gradually slide into our life: I knew alcoholism was a problem for many Belarusians. My agitation was based, in part, on personal experience: my older sister and brother had been alcohol abusers, causing much heartache to their families. Also, my grandfather was a heavy drinker who committed suicide. Understandably, I had little tolerance for alcohol abuse. I would simply not allow it to be a part of my life.

The next morning, I raised the issue.

"Walter, Larysa put on a lovely party last night. But the drinking was too much. That Director was clearly trying to get you as plastered as he was."

"That seems a little exaggerated," Walter responded, in an ameliorating manner – which only irritated me more. Then he explained his stance: "I was aware, before coming to Munich, that alcoholism was a problem here. So I let it be known that I'm not a drinker. Maybe you didn't notice that, when they were toasting us, I barely tipped the glass."

I'd seen several refills and wasn't totally buying that explanation, so I replied,

"Okay, fine, but you need to know, if drinking becomes the norm, I'm leaving. That's not what I married into, and it's not what I want in my life."

"Oh, come on!" Walter responded. I could see he was getting exasperated with me. I had had enough of the discussion also, so I coldly turned and walked out, slamming the apartment door behind me.

Walking off my self-righteousness in the street, I began rehashing the last few minutes. When I stopped at a café for a cup of comfort food, thick hot chocolate with whipped cream, I started to calm down. How could I have told Walter that I'd leave? I was beginning to feel disappointed with myself for letting the situation get so out of hand and unhappy that our noticeable disagreement at the party had *not* made the good first impression I'd hoped for. I also wondered if we would have to set new parameters for our relationship here.

Once back in the apartment, I headed for the kitchen to make lunch.

"What are you making? That smells good," Walter said, just like nothing had happened.

Later on, he quietly said, "I had a good time last night, but I'm sorry if the drinking bothered you. I can assure you, I'm not going to be the Director's drinking partner," he chuckled. Then he added, "Now, how about going for a long hike in the country this afternoon? Get some nice fresh air in us, eh?" I knew he was redirecting, but I felt reassured that he understood my concerns.

Dangers could be internally generated, I'd come to realize, as well as coming from politically opposing forces. I determined not to let either one overwhelm me – but I could see that I'd have to keep alert to the early signs, so that I could offset the possible consequences.

Brother George (r), with friends, at refugee camp

5
TRACES OF WORLD WAR II

Not surprisingly, World War II became more real to me while living in Europe. We saw in Munich, first-hand, some of the physical, as well as psychological, effects of the war.

I tried to adjust my American perspective by viewing things around me from a German or historical point of view. For instance, there were high hills with gas vents outside of Munich, in the midst of flat farm fields. They were much like the vents I'd seen in New Jersey garbage dumps. Underneath those hills, I was told, were piles of rubble left from the Allied bombing of Munich.

I visualized the residents of Munich dragging the remnants of their city to these dumps – and the anger and animosity that they must have felt. I was just a pre-teen during the war, but I felt guilty when the Allies destroyed whole German cities, like Munich, rather than just bombing the industrial sections. Of course, the German attempt to destroy London came to mind as one explanation. Maybe the Allies did it to demoralize the Germans, I thought, with the hope of shortening the war – but it smacked of unnecessary vengeance to me.

Munich could have been quickly rebuilt, in a modern style. But I was glad that the city officials had restored most of the centuries-old buildings, recapturing their original Bavarian charm. One attraction for tourists, for instance, was watching the parading figures in the reconstructed Glockenspiel clock that chimed twice a day in the Marienplatz town square.

All around us were many reminders of the war. Once, we visited Hitler's Eagle's Nest, high up on the pinnacle of a mountain near Berchtesgaden. As I looked out at the green valley far below, I recalled a movie that showed Hitler ensconced there with his generals and henchmen, planning some of their worst Nazi deeds. It was a beautiful location, but for me it was tarnished by its previous purpose.

We also visited Dachau, the prototype for concentration camps, just outside of Munich. We walked through the barracks and viewed the photo exhibits, which showed the emaciated inmates. I was overwhelmingly depressed, thinking about the 25,000 people who had died in Dachau – even without the use of gas chambers.

For some time after that trip, when I looked at older Munich residents, I wondered whether they'd supported the Nazis, simply kept quiet, or been themselves persecuted.

Most of our contacts with Germans were positive. Certainly, young Germans were homogenizing with other young people around the world, as reflected in their interest in Seattle grunge music and computers.

But sometimes, when older Germans learned we were Americans, their faces would take on stern, steely looks. Trying to think from their perspective, I wondered if they had a photo on their bureau of a husband or relative who hadn't come back from the war. Maybe they were remembering the American bombers destroying their home. Or perhaps their national pride was hurt, since Germany had been defeated and yet still had American troops stationed there, 40 years later.

I could understand the reasons for the negative behavior toward us, though it was uncomfortable being disliked just because I was an American. That experience was later reflected in my having a special empathy for foreigners and consciously trying to include them in conversations.

Walter always added a deep historical perspective to our trips, and I appreciated gaining a better understanding of Europe from him. Europeans, in general, seemed to know history so much more intimately than Americans. And, of course, Walter had lived through some of that history himself.

On one trip we visited several locations where Walter had lived with his family as a Displaced Person, for four years after the war. His family was part of the surge of thousands of European refugees, either fleeing Soviet persecution or simply displaced by the war. Besides Walter, his family included his older brother George, his younger brother Bill, and his parents.

I asked Walter to share with me what it was like during those uncertain years. He said that in one D.P. location in Germany, a bombed-out Messerschmidt factory, he sometimes walked down the hall and jumped out onto piles of empty ruins.

Later, we stopped in Wurzburg to see the motorcycle garage where refugee families had put up blankets for privacy between the assigned double bunks. At other times, he said, the family was lodged in workers' housing. Fortunately, by then, UNRRA (the

United Nations Relief and Rehabilitation Administration) supplied some of their basic needs.

"It was an exciting day when Red Cross packages arrived in camp," Walter said. "Often we ate in a common mess, but sometimes we were given a hotplate for cooking on our own. I remember once scrounging for utensils in a nearby bombed-out factory cafeteria."

Walter said that his family's life in the camps wasn't as bad as for some. His mother, as Mary Novak, had been one of a group of Czech girls who'd won scholarships to attend Vassar College, so she was fluent in English. Consequently, she was able to work in the U.N. relief agency and provide some minimal income for the family during that time.

It was interesting to me that Walter remembered those years as a time of freedom and gaining teenage independence from parental control. For two years, when he was 13 and 14, he was either away from the family in a YMCA summer camp or living in a dormitory at a Belarusian school. Evidently, there wasn't much supervision at the school. He recalled persuading others to skip classes with him to go down by the river for adventures. His stories confirmed that he had an independent streak and was considered somewhat of a mischief maker in his youth.

Now, Walter realizes how his parents must have worried about the family's future, but – at the time – he and his brothers were mainly concerned with sports, scouting activities, and girls. Yet, I wondered what lasting impact such an itinerant life might leave on an impressionable teen.

The turning point for the family came when President Truman signed a bill to let additional war refugees enter the United States, beyond the limited quotas. Then, the family of a former Vassar schoolmate of Mary's agreed to sponsor them into the United States. Thus, in 1949, they traveled to Bremerhaven to board a military transport ship, the USS *General Harry Taylor*, bound for New York City.

After hearing about others' hardships, it was embarrassing to think how easy those war years had been for me on our farm. Since we raised almost everything we needed, rationing hardly affected us. We had had air raid drills at school, but the closest we came to war was the rumor of a Japanese submarine sighting off Puget Sound. Now, I was gaining a new perspective on WW II.

Munich Christmas Market

6
COPING WITH A NEW LIFESTYLE

During the fall of 1988, I focused on trying to find a new rhythm for my life. In America, I'd found it very comforting that my life had a routine: Monday was laundry day; after-school time was for the boys; and grocery shopping was done in one large supermarket, once a week. There, I had been deeply involved with the children's activities, evening business meetings, and organizational events.

Now, daily routines seemed to consume all my time. Laundry had to wait for Walter's day off, so he could help lug it to the local *Wascherei*, and shopping became a major undertaking.

Groceries were now purchased every two or three days. In the States, I cooked several meals at once, freezing some for later. Having only a tiny freezer in Munich, we instead ate more prepared meals and ate out more often. I was grateful that Munich had many international restaurants: Czech, Thai, Italian, Argentine steak houses, and others. Across the bridge from the Radios was a typical Gasthaus, Herzog Park Quelle, with blue and white Bavarian flags hanging around the door. It was less expensive than other restaurants, so we often ate there.

The Bavarian *"Gruess Gott"* (good day), instead of the more formal German *"Guten Tag,"* always greeted us as we entered. We preferred a table in a quiet corner, near an open window – to avoid some of the disadvantages: the air inside was heavy with cigarette smoke, and the loud talking at the Stammtisch table was frequently punctuated with sudden guffawing at bawdy jokes.

We had to adjust to different foods in Germany. Walter usually ordered pork, sauerkraut, and potato dumplings. I more often opted for venison, topped with wild mushroom gravy, whipped cream, and tart *preiselberries* (similar to cranberries). For dessert, flaky, warm apple strudel almost always capped the evening.

Besides the frequent local shopping in Schwabing, about once a week I took the U-bahn subway to downtown Munich. This was a typical shopping trip:

I got up early so that I could enjoy a non-American breakfast at Donisl: Weisswurst. It's a delicate, white veal sausage, made with parsley and served in a pot of water, with a special sweet mustard and salty pretzels on the side. I ordered my favorite Apfelschorle drink to accompany it. Then, I stopped at Rischart, a large bakery with an attached café, and bought their rich almond breakfast pastry, with a gooey marzipan center, for Walter's breakfast the next day.

My third stop was the Dallmayr delicatessen, with its inviting nooks of different foods, all prepared with scrumptious spices. I didn't stop there too often, because Walter felt the prices were exorbitant – though the delicious food seemed worth it to me. His "watching of pennies" is probably a good balance to my

Depression-inspired attitude: "I don't want to have to always be thinking about the cost of things." I'm not always happy about this counterpoint; it's been a source of contention at times.

The next stop was the *Viktualienmarkt*, a farmer's market held in a large square, near the center of Munich. I enjoyed how picturesque it was, with its blue and white checkered Bavarian banners flying atop the tent-like market stalls. Most of the produce came from nearby farms and was therefore very fresh.

The *Kartoffel Handlung* potato stall amazed me – it offered 11 different shapes, sizes, and colors of potatoes. And I could hardly believe how many stalls there were just for sausages: Knackwurst, Nuernberger Bratwurst, Wienerwurst, Frankfurters, Blutwurst, Mettwurst – many were "wursts" that I'd never heard of before. In some ways, the Viktualienmarkt was even better than the famous Pike Place Market where I loved to shop in Seattle, when we went "back home" to my family. It seemed to help, to relate life here to what I'd known before.

I wrestled with the amount of time needed just for shopping. It seemed to me that my talents could be used more productively elsewhere. Though I had to admit that I didn't have something else to do just yet.

Sunday was the main day available for us to explore Munich, and we found some more sophisticated attractions of the city, beyond its provincial Bavarian charm: museums, galleries, concerts, and even an English-language movie theatre, Museum Lichtspiel.

One warm October evening, Walter and I strolled around the streets of Schwabing, where we joined the crowd of Muenchners browsing the galleries and sitting in outdoor cafes. It was a weekend, so there were tables set up along Leopoldstrasse, with artists selling their paintings and jewelry. We stopped to watch the kibitzing of those gathered around a chess table. It struck me that Schwabing was like Greenwich Village, where I'd lived for a year after first arriving in New York City from college in the Midwest. It had the same friendly, artistic atmosphere.

That evening, I commented to Walter, "Munich is a perfect-sized city: it's small enough to navigate easily, yet has so much to offer." He agreed.

Then the Munich winter set in, with its dreary overcast cloud cover, rain, and slushy snow. I didn't go out as much and began to feel isolated and depressed. Sometimes, I'd come home from shopping and break down into tears – not from unhappiness so much, but rather to relieve the tension of navigating my way through the day in a foreign land.

One day I was feeling desperate to speak to someone in English. But Walter waved me off, saying, "Let's talk about that later; I have to finish reading this material now." I understood that he had to catch up with those colleagues who'd been onsite for years at the Radios. And, of course, my conversation wasn't very significant, compared to all the political changes in Eastern Europe.

I just needed a few words, or a reassuring hug. I felt left out of Walter's world. I missed the close cooperation we'd had in our business back home. At that point, tears flooded my eyes, and I knew I needed to shift the focus of my thinking. This was the essence of my inner conversation that day:

Okay Joanne, you have to accept that you're not going to be working closely with Walter, as you did in the States. Stop looking back. See how you can build the foundation of a new relationship. Obviously, you're often going to be operating in separate realms here. So, maybe you'll need to play a more supporting role when he has questions or problems and an outside perspective might be helpful.

That night, I picked up a religious journal and read an uplifting article about peace and contentment coming from within and not being dependent on outside circumstances or people. I carried those thoughts to bed.

The next morning dawned with golden sunshine coming through the shuttered windows. Optimism charged me with energy. I decided to focus just on the good happening in my new, exciting life, rather than on what seemed to be missing.

Since Walter was so busy with his work, one practical idea was to organize activities for us on his days off. I started looking for special events that would give us fun memories of our time in Munich. And I planned weekend trips outside of the city to enrich our experience of Europe.

Winter, itself, did offer some unexpected choices. For instance, the Christmas Market, held on the downtown pedestrian mall in Munich, was a special treat that brought joy to alleviate winter doldrums. Walter and I wrapped up warmly in scarves and down jackets and meandered in and out of the crowds, gazing at the beautiful Christmas decorations in the outdoor stalls. Steam escaped Walter's lips as he sipped the hot *Gluhwein* (mulled wine), and I munched on roasted chestnuts from a sidewalk grill. Strolling musicians added to the fairytale atmosphere, along with the sweet fragrance of hot candy-coated almonds.

Christmas was lonely, however. We didn't have enough money to fly back to be with our boys – the house still hadn't sold. I saw an ad for a bus trip to Oberndorf, Austria to spend Christmas Eve at a chapel associated with the writing of *Silent Night*. It was a clear, starry night when we arrived at the small white chapel on a lonely hill. Then, just at the stroke of midnight, we huddled inside and began to sing *Stille Nacht*. It was a deeply moving and reverent European Christmas.

For another break in the winter, we rented a car to go skiing in the Mattrei area of the Austrian Alps. The area had a storybook appearance with small, snow-covered, steep-roofed chalets scattered about the ridges. I could visualize one of my favorite childhood book characters, Heidi, skipping along in her dirndl skirt, looking for her gruff grandfather. Skiing on those open slopes gave me a feeling of great freedom.

Visitors from the States also helped me feel still connected to our old life. One visitor was my friend Bonnie. She brought her new husband, Bill, who was eager to visit the Radios, where he'd worked during the more CIA-related days.

By spring, our trips outside Munich expanded our horizons even more. We rented a car for a drive to Starnberger See. We drove around the large lake, watching sailboats quietly drifting along on the slightly ruffled waves, and I spied a golden church steeple, glistening with sunlight, on a far-off shore. We stopped at an open-air hotel café that had a band and twirled to old-fashioned waltzes, tangos, and polkas until dusk.

The next week, I suggested that we go hiking – a favorite weekend past-time of most Germans.

"Good idea," Walter said. "Larysa has a home near Schliersee, in the foothills of the Alps. She recently invited us to visit her. Let me check with her about this weekend. We could hike one of those *wandern* trails that are all around her mountain lake."

We ended up not only going, but buying two interestingly carved walking sticks, warm Alpine sweaters, and sturdy hiking shoes. We were beginning to look like our Bavarian counterparts!

I greeted the coming summer with happy anticipation of more local outings and a vacation trip behind the Iron Curtain.

Czech relatives at lake cottage

7
GOING BEHIND THE IRON CURTAIN

The summer of 1989 was our first in Europe. We were surprised to hear that the Radios gave six weeks of vacation time, starting with the first year. For three of those six weeks, we were taking a trip into Eastern Europe, to visit Walter's relatives in Czechoslovakia and Poland.

We'd learned to set goals in our business, and we applied that idea to our lives as well. So, for this trip, I asked myself, What is the purpose of this activity? What would I like to see as an outcome? On the Czech part of our trip, I anticipated meeting Walter's relatives and seeing where his pre-teen years were spent – hoping that would help me to understand my European husband better. I also wanted to get a clearer sense of what life under Communism was like.

I thought I'd conquered most of my earlier fears about going behind the Iron Curtain. However, a few days before we left, a news story came over the TV about a Soviet spy being exchanged for an American tourist, arrested as a CIA agent. I knew RFE/RL had been started with CIA money, although now it was funded directly by the U.S. Congress. I'd also heard that the Soviets still considered Radios' personnel to be affiliated with the CIA. I wondered, What might that portend for us?

As our departure neared, Walter said, "Joanne, I hear that the hotels in Eastern Europe are pretty decrepit. I think we'd be better off renting a motor home and driving in; then, at least, we'd always have a decent place to sleep."

"That sounds like a great idea! We wouldn't have the hassle of unpacking every night, and maybe we'd also less likely be followed." Walter grimaced at my statement; he'd already berated me for that concern.

The German motor home we rented was short at 22 feet, but included everything we needed: kitchen, table, bath, and bed, and it would be easy to drive and park. The one negative thing, though, was that Walter's Radios supervisor said we were going to be the first RFE/RL personnel allowed to *drive* behind the Iron Curtain. That idea made me feel uneasy, as if we were being sent out to test Glasnost.

As I packed the motor home, I thought about how conditions might be in the East. Not wanting to seem like the proverbial rich American, I chose simple clothing. Besides bedding and food, we added a crate of apples and some medicine Walter's aunt requested. I made sure I had my Bible and other spiritual sustenance. Also important was the camera. We wanted to get memorable shots of the relatives – just in case Glasnost was reversed, and we couldn't return to see them again.

Then, at the last minute, I ran back into the house to get a notebook and pencils. It had just hit me that this trip was a unique opportunity. My journalism training compelled me to take detailed notes. Even if our trip would only be shared with friends and relatives, I wanted it to be captured as accurately as possible.

We hoped for no delays along the way, since we wanted to arrive at the relatives' summer cottage before dark. Walter said it should be a five hour trip from Munich to Prague. Unfortunately, he hadn't figured into the equation time lost to border backups and the possibility of special treatment.

We waited in line for over two hours at the Waidhaus-Rozvadov border crossing between Germany and Czechoslovakia. As we got closer, we saw many border guards who frowned and looked forbidding in their dark uniforms. There was definitely no laughter, no easy joie de vivre, as we'd seen recently on the Italian border.

Finally, it was our turn. A guard took our passports back to a little hut and made a phone call. Another guard, who spoke in broken English, told us, haltingly,

"Pull to side and wait." And there we waited, and waited.

"After all we've gone through, do you think we now might be turned away at the border?" I asked Walter, with a sigh of frustration.

Suddenly, there was a knock on the motor home door. A stocky guard pointed a raised submachine gun at us, motioning for us to get out. He searched every cabinet and cranny of the motor home, even inside the cereal boxes. We stood there awkwardly, trying to look innocent and unconcerned. Finally, the first guard came out with our passports, nodded to the English-speaking guard, and we were allowed to continue on our trip.

As we traveled along, at first I saw a swath of emptiness on the hilly border. Thousands of evergreen trees had been cut and replaced by crossed stanchions, barbed wire, and what looked like electrified wire on top. Two guards marched along the border in tandem. These were all grim reminders to not cross this border uninvited.

Then, a small town came into view: a shocking sight. It still looked like a war-torn area, more than 40 years after the war. The homes were dingy and had obviously been left unpainted ever since. Parts of many houses were sagging and badly patched. Some even had pockmarks from long-past gunfire. The one brightening effect was the flowers, planted by caring residents doing the one life-affirming thing still within their control.

On the street, people looked dispirited, as if they were mentally hunched over by the daily burden of oppression.

As we entered the outskirts of the first large city, Pilsen, we saw monoliths of concrete slab apartment buildings looming together, in drab, gray rows. Streets were filthy and rutted; old signs were peeling and hard to read. There were streetcars, but few automobiles, except for occasional black sedans used by Communist government officials.

Up a hill, I was relieved to see a sign with an arrow pointing toward *"Praha"* (Prague), taking us out of Pilsen. As we neared larger villages we saw a yellow-gray haze of pollution. Then, as we approached Prague, it got worse, and my eyes started to sting. Later, we learned that schools in Prague were sometimes closed in winter, and parents were advised to keep their children indoors because of the severe pollution from burning soft-brown coal.

Suddenly, I panicked. "Walter, where's the paper with the directions to their cottage? . . . Oh, it's here. How come we're not meeting them in Prague first, since we're going right by it?"

"This way, we don't have to report to the police and get into the system right away. We'll have the weekend to talk and relax with the family by the lake first. That's why they told us to come on Friday."

I fixated on "report to the police." So they *are* going to be tracking us?

As we drove around the outskirts of Prague and started toward the *chata* (cottage), I saw that we'd entered a scenic vacation area with rolling hills, rivers, evergreen trees, and tranquil lakes with small houses on their shores. We turned off the highway toward the village of Vyzlovka, bumped down a rutted gravel road, and finally got to what we hoped was their summer cottage. The travails of the trip were now replaced by the anticipation of meeting Walter's relatives.

The family had been watching for us. Little three-year-old Petia came running down the path, only to stop midway in the driveway, where he stood frozen in awe of the strangers driving toward him in a big motor home. He turned around and then hid behind his mother's skirt for the next hour. His mother, our second cousin Andulka (Anna), was slim, dark-haired, and had large, serious brown eyes. She seemed shy, especially with me, since she didn't know much English.

Andulka's mother, our cousin Helenka (Helena), hurried past the others to open the gate to allow our motor home to enter the long driveway. Helenka greeted us with smiles, but she looked somewhat wary at the same time.

Then, Aunt Anichka's round face came into view. She was beaming upon seeing her sister Mary's middle son's return, after so many years in America. Anichka greeted us with *"Dobry Den"* (Good day) and continued with a flow of excited conversation. Walter haltingly answered in some of his half-remembered Czech phrases. We hugged and headed for the house. I noted the neighbor's eyes watching from her window as we passed.

Their chata was a charmingly quaint European cottage made of white stucco (now streaked with grey soot) with a long, sloping red-tiled roof, rounded alcoves, and dark brown wooden shutters. The cottage was designed and built by Walter's Uncle Frantishek, an architect and engineer. In its prime, the chata was known in the village as *pernikova chaloupka* (the Gingerbread House) because it stood out among the more simple, camp-like buildings in the neighborhood.

The inside of the cottage seemed old-fashioned. In the kitchen was a sink, with running cold water, and a small wood-burning stove. The living area had a built-in dining alcove, from which we stepped down into a living room. A wood-burning stove in the corner was the source of heat in the house. I was charmed by the view. Windows looked out onto a yard sloping toward a quiet lake surrounded by trees.

Walter later explained to me about housing in Czechoslovakia. Czech citizens could no longer own their main residences in the city. After the Communist takeover, the government often assigned others to share those residences with their previous owners.

(Later, my Czech friend, Suzana, told me of her remembrances of how the government kept close tabs on its citizens. She said that her home sheltered several families of cousins during the Communist years. In the basement apartment, the government placed an informer whose role was to clean the rooms of the home and check the contents for anything not acceptable to the government. Suzana said, "As a child, I thought it was strange that my parents always closed the windows whenever we were having a serious discussion." Obviously, it was an attempt to prevent the informer from overhearing what was said.)

As a political tactic, the Czechoslovak government allowed most citizens to keep occupancy of their small summer cottages, weekend camping sites, or garden plots. Evidently, this policy had kept many residents happy and away from the city on weekends when, in some Communist-controlled countries, gatherings in the city became protests. I was grateful that the relatives had had this cottage retreat for their extended family.

On Friday evening, the working men arrived. Mirek, Helenka's strapping and dynamic husband, had a booming voice. Petr was Andulka's smiling, blond husband. Tall, serious Mira was Andulka's brother. I was relieved: both Mirek and Petr spoke quite good English. My conversation with them, however, was circumspect, because I wasn't certain of their political leanings.

Later that evening, Walter and I explored the three small upstairs bedrooms, one of which became ours. Since there was no heat at night, we were grateful for the thick down comforters. Glancing into the tiny bathroom, we were advised that the toilet was not working, so we'd have to pour water into it. "It's not possible to get the parts to fix it," someone explained.

As we retired, Walter recalled times at the cottage and in Prague 40 years before. "Besides Aunt Anichka, I remember mother's sister, Aunt Lidushka; and her brother, Uncle Jarka; and Anichka's husband, Uncle Frantishek – all who are no longer with us. They treated us Stankievich kids as the children they never had. They provided us with a real sense of having an extended family." (Anichka's daughter, Helenka, and her brother were adopted into the family later.)

"But, during the war years," I asked, "weren't conditions pretty bad here?"

"Actually, the Czech lands were an island of tranquility, compared to most of war-torn Europe. They had been taken over by the Germans, essentially without any fighting. We just went about our business. At our young age, what we remembered were trips to the theatre and amusement parks and vacations on working farms and summer camps. I recall those three years with fondness."

I was eager to hear more, but it was late, and Walter was tired from driving, so he said he'd tell me more another time.

The next evening was memorable. We cooked sausage on wooden sticks, over a dug-out fire pit, while we talked and sang. Mirek organized the fire building, directing different family members in what to do. He was obviously the head of the family. The evening was joyous, but also quite tranquil, looking out on the setting sun over the lake.

It made me think of our own family outdoor cookouts back in New Jersey with our sons. Our home had a lovely wooded back yard and a lake across the street, not too dissimilar. Picnics there usually included hamburgers and chicken cooked on our deck grill, with potato salad and carrot sticks, and brownies for dessert. It was always a happy family time. I missed our boys, but I was also developing a new sense of close family ties in Czechoslovakia, as we huddled around the fire together.

Political satire with Prague puppeteer

8
EXPLORING PRAGUE

Before our trip, Prague had been just another European capital to me. As we headed into the city on Sunday evening, I anticipated a few days of exploring its touted Old-World charm.

We stayed at Aunt Anichka's apartment, since she was the only one we were legitimately supposed to visit. I was glad to see that her apartment was in a pleasant, several-storied building, rather than one of the high, ugly, concrete complexes. Her building even had a garden at the back.

As we opened the door of her first-floor apartment, I was surprised to see several inches of heavy padding covering the inside of the door. Later, when we were alone with Anichka, she quietly, but defiantly, admitted,

"I listen to the short-wave Czech broadcasts on Radio Free

Europe almost every day, but I keep it at a low volume. Even if the house informer overhears and reports it, I'm an old woman. What can they do to me?"

Anichka's apartment was frayed-looking. Old curtains hung at the windows, sofa seats sagged, and tables were chipped and marked with years of use. But there was still the hint of a former well-to-do status: furniture made of expensive wood and several beautiful vases and artifacts. Books were everywhere. For our visit, she had added a touch of color, a vase of flowers on the dining room table.

On Monday morning, Aunt Anichka accompanied Walter to Prague's central police station to register us as foreign guests in the city – a strict requirement.

Later that day, Petr, Cousin Andulka's husband, took us on a tour of Prague. He was charming and discussed the sights fluently in English. Petr was now an attorney, but he had spent college summers teaching tennis in Switzerland, where he learned to speak English at the resorts. Our conversations that day were purposely kept nonpolitical.

Petr was an excellent guide. He obviously loved his city and knew its history. Though dark and grimy, the Old Town beautifully combined Gothic, Baroque, and Renaissance architecture, unmarred by the presence of modern buildings. I loved all the sights: the towers that seemed to be chopped off at the top; the tall, thin church spires reaching toward the heavens; frescoes and statues on buildings and bridges; the gold-festooned palaces; and the arches and covered arcades. The wide Vltava River, winding through the center of town, offered an open vista to the Hradcany Castle hill, otherwise hidden by the narrow streets. The narrow, winding cobblestone alleyways leading up the castle hill augmented the feeling of our walking in an ancient past.

The next morning, Aunt Anichka gave us a city map, and we struck out on our own to sightsee. Since Walter knew some of the language, we dared to seek out the "unabridged version" of the city. Our experience was strikingly different from the day before.

As we came out of the Andel subway stop, we saw the part of the city where townspeople lived and shopped. Walter translated the names of the shops: "food store" and "restaurant." These generic names reminded me that the shops were all government-run.

This bleak truth was matched by the scarce and nearly inedible food offered in the stores. The only vegetables we found were a few sturdy cabbage heads, some potatoes with blooming eyes, and limp carrots. Apples were wrinkled and half-rotten, and there was no citrus fruit at all. The meat store was even worse. There, long lines of people waited to buy a single sausage and some cold cuts, but there was no other meat available. I cringed at the vast disparity between Prague's stores and our overflowing American supermarkets.

I felt so bad for Walter's relatives, who had lived for 40 years with such limited choices. But then, I realized, the limitation wasn't only in food options. The limitations also extended to travel outside of the Soviet Bloc, to the kinds of assigned work the government allowed, to their freedom to express themselves without fear of serious consequences, and in many other ways.

After several rides on public transportation, I realized that I'd seen the same man in a blue coat at least twice before on different trams. Easing close to my husband, I whispered,

"I think we're being followed by the man in the blue coat. He's been on several trams and subways with us."

"Oh, Joanne, I'm sure that's not true. You're probably just imaging that," replied my imperturbable husband. But I felt certain I was right.

After we got off the tram, we walked downtown. Wenceslas

Square swept impressively before us up the hill, five blocks to the imposing National Museum and statue of King Wenceslas on his horse. At the bottom of the hill, we discovered one of the well-known political puppeteers. Walter translated the puppeteer's story, explaining how the double and triple entendres had deeper political and satirical meaning than did the children's story on the surface. Many of the people who gathered around and chuckled to themselves were, in fact, adults.

I intuitively guessed which person in the crowd was there as the official minder. He seemed to be observing the attendees, rather than watching the performers. But I didn't say anything to Walter about the observer, as I'd had enough put-downs for my "imaginings".

I felt frustrated that Walter couldn't seem to accredit my intuitions. I wasn't sure if this stemmed from his engineering training, or his general discomfort with anything not observable. For me, those intuitions had so often proven right that they seemed even more dependable than human reasoning. I decided to accept our differences on this matter and recognize that perhaps we were a good complement to each other.

As we came out of the subway, back at the Andel stop, we started down Walter's proverbial memory lane. He became excited to visit places from his childhood: his old school, still open after 50 years; the blocked-off side street where he played soccer with friends; the steep hill he'd climbed with his older brother George; and the busy cross street near their apartment, where Walter often took the hand of his little brother Bill to ensure his safe crossing. Walter's voice rose with animation as he viewed these locations and memories flooded in.

Walter pointed at the apartment house on Na Zatlance, the street where the four of them lived during that earlier period. He wanted to visit the cousin's apartment, to see how it had changed. But when we were at the lake they'd said that it would be better for them if we, as Americans, did not visit them in the city.

The apartment house was a sturdy, five-story building, built by one uncle's construction company and owned by another uncle, the doctor. But, since being taken over by the government, decades of disrepair had left their mark. Everything seemed just the way it was – which was good for Walter's memories, but not so good for the building.

Since Walter seemed transported back to his childhood, I asked him to continue telling me about his life in Prague during the war.

"Walter, you shared some of the good memories with the relatives, but what do you remember about the German occupation?"

He said, "I saw German soldiers on the streets and sensed resentment toward them from adults in the family. It wasn't too repressive, though, at least until after Heydrich's killing. Then the Germans really cracked down." (That was in May of 1942, when Czech soldiers from London parachuted in to kill Reinhard Heydrich, the top-ranking S.S. officer in Prague. In retaliation, the Germans obliterated the nearby town of Lidice.)

In town, Walter said he saw German posters vilifying Americans, Jews, and the Bolsheviks. He said, "I didn't know much about Americans, and our interactions with Jews in Vilnia had been positive, but the assessment about the Bolsheviks seemed to be supported by our family's bad experiences with them. From our family's standpoint, the greater fear was of the Soviets, not the Germans. Father had tried to form an underground Belarus party, and was now considered an enemy of the state by the Soviets."

I said, "It must have been awful for your mother, during those years, not knowing if her husband was even alive."

"Sometimes he was able to get a message to us. And toward the end of the war, Father joined us for a short time. But, when he heard that Soviet troops were approaching Prague, he left, crossing into Germany to seek safety in the American zone."

The family's plan had been for Walter's father to rejoin them in Prague, once the Soviet troops left Czechoslovakia. That plan changed drastically, a few months later, when a KGB officer, accompanied by two Soviet soldiers, knocked on their door. The officer demanded,

"Where is your husband, Jan Stankievich?"

Walter's mother was so upset she was shaking, and she stammered, "I divorced him." She hoped that the officers would, then, allow her to stay with her family in Czechoslovakia.

But when the other officer started looking around, he opened a closet door and saw a large coat and men's shoes, evidence that her husband had been there.

"We'll be back," the officer stated.

Having heard what had happened to others, she understood that the consequences could mean the family being "sent back," possibly to a Gulag. The Soviets had put up signs in Prague: "All people from territories under Soviet control in 1939 (which then included Vilnia) must report for repatriation."

That night, after consulting with her brother, Mary prepared the four of them to flee quickly over the border toward Pilsen, in the American zone. As they arrived by train at the demarcation line, the Soviets checked one set of railroad cars, the Americans the other. Walter saw his mother's fear as she watched the Soviet soldiers marching along the tracks. "But we were lucky," he said. "It was the Americans who checked our papers and allowed us to continue."

Eventually, the family arrived at a Displaced Persons camp in Germany, and they were able to find their father and live together there, for four years.

The family still had hope of going back to either Prague or Vilnia "when the Soviets left," but they soon understood that wasn't going to happen. They were forced to look for another place to establish a home and finally found refuge in America.

On our last night in Prague the family gathered at Anichka's apartment for dinner with us. Despite everyone's quiet entrance, the downstairs neighbor kept opening his door to check the comings and goings.

During the evening, conversation seemed awkward. I wondered, If I were to ask a simple question such as, "What kind of work do you do?" might it be suspected that we would report the answer to someone? After all, reporting and being reported upon was part of their experience. I decided that it was safer to let Walter carry most of the conversation. He could focus on the good memories they'd had together.

We ended the evening, and our Czech visit, with warm good-bye hugs. It would have been normal to say "Come visit us," but regrettably that was not possible. The Communist government usually did not allow more than one member of a family to travel outside the country at a time – with the rest of the family held as virtual hostages, to prevent defections.

Although I'd recently worried that Walter and I were leading somewhat separate lives, this trip made me feel closer to him. I gained a better appreciation of how his childhood had shaped his thinking. For one thing, since the family could never take much with them from one war experience to the next, he'd never cared much about things or appearances. Understandably, then, Walter didn't see much reason to spend money on expensive furnishings and lovely artifacts – which I yearned for, as living in a beautiful environment was important to me.

I later admitted to Walter that there hadn't been any dire experiences to disturb us in Czechoslovakia; it was, rather, an accumulation of minor, negative impressions. They made me feel like there was just a scent of danger wafting in the air – not totally identifiable, but enough to put me on guard. I wondered if we'd feel the same sense of oppression in the next part of our trip, in Poland.

Belarusian relatives in Czaplinek

9
CONNECTING WITH RELATIVES IN POLAND

The first goal of our Polish trip was to meet Walter's Belarusian relatives, who lived in the northwest seaport of Szczecin.

"Why do so many of your Belarusian relatives live in Poland, rather than in Belarus?" I asked Walter, as we started for the border.

He explained that after serfdom was abolished in the Russian Empire in the 19th century, peasants could buy land from the state, and the Stankievich family bought a small farm.

"The successive Stankievich generations tended their farm near Arlianaty, in the Vilnia region, through the upheavals of two world wars and often-changing borders. Of Father's generation, his younger brother, Stanley, immigrated early on to Connecticut, and Father only reluctantly immigrated to the United States after World War II, when his Belarusian activism made it dangerous for him to stay in Soviet-controlled countries. Father's two sisters, Amilia and Ewa, married local Belarusian farmers – and most of their families were the ones to leave later for Poland."

Walter recounted how it happened. After the war, Ewa and her husband were allowed to leave Belarus (then almost fully within the Soviet Union) as part of a population exchange program. Their new farm in Poland was in "recovered lands," which had been occupied by Germans. Ewa's married daughter, Jozefa, and her family, were only able to leave Belarus during the next "thaw" in 1957, after the death of Stalin.

"What about the other sister, Amilia?" I asked.

"She died in 1958. But her daughter, Hanna, joined the cousins in Poland, after years in Soviet "gulag" camps in Siberia. Amelia's politically active older son, Stas, immigrated to the United States with his family after WW II. Juzik, his younger brother, suffered much harassment from the KGB because of Stas's activism, and he finally took some of his family and crossed the border into Lithuania." (After the breakup of the Soviet Union, Walter was in touch with Juzik's son, Vaclov Stankevich, who'd been elected to the Lithuanian Parliament.)

"That's the saga of my relatives," Walter said, tossing a hand in the air and chuckling with embarrassment about his long-windedness. "All of them are now spread over three continents, and in at least seven countries."

"Whoa," I said, "that's even more exciting than my father going into Indian Territory to homestead!"

As we neared the border, I stopped thinking about Walter's family, and turned my attention to Poland. I wondered, Will life there be pretty much the same as what we've seen in Czechoslovakia? "The Monolith of Communism" was a phrase I'd heard often. It implied a uniformity of atheism, total police control, and informers everywhere. But would that be the case?

I knew that Czechoslovakia had a different political situation, with Soviet troops still stationed there since the Prague Spring, whereas in Poland their own forces were in control. Also, of course, there were different histories and different ethnic characteristics. For instance, I'd always thought of Poles as being generally assertive, while Czechs seemed quite gentle. However, the Communist leaders of Eastern European countries all seemed to be the same kind of older, hard-line dictatorial types, not appearing too interested in participating in Gorbachev's Glasnost.

Crossing the border from Czechoslovakia into Poland was an expected ordeal. There were long lines and extra scrutiny of our motor home and passports.

As we left the border, I began to recognize contrasts with what we'd seen in Czechoslovakia. The Polish farms appeared smaller, with a variety of crops, and they seemed more cared for than the huge Czech collectives. I saw a farmer tilling the land with a small plow, pulled by an ox. A woman, probably his wife, with a long peasant skirt and kerchief, was trudging out with his lunch. I wondered out loud why these farms looked more productive than the collectives in Czechoslovakia.

Walter explained, "Polish farmers were very resistant to having their farms collectivized, and many were allowed to keep ownership, though many of their crops are requisitioned by the state."

Farmers producing their own food, however, did not translate into more food in the stores. For instance, since we often ate in the motor home, we needed to replenish our supplies at times. One day we stopped in a small town. There were just a few stores, and we were happy to find a meat market. I opened the store's door, and then looked back at Walter with a "you've-got-to-be-kidding" roll of the eyes. The petite, blond saleslady stood behind the counter, displaying the three pieces of meat available. We gratefully bought one large sausage. Then, we took a photo of the nearly empty store. We figured no one would believe such scarcity otherwise.

On Sunday, as we drove through another small town, I couldn't see much difference from the towns we'd seen in Czechoslovakia. Houses were in disrepair, and apartment buildings were drab concrete *panelaks* (buildings put up quickly with slabs of concrete). But one sight got my attention: crowds of people standing in the rain, outside the Catholic Church.

"Look at this," I nudged Walter, "I thought Communists were atheists!"

"Not Poles," he said, sounding a bit surprised at my ignorance. "The Catholic Church is very powerful here. Some of the clergy have caved in to Communist control, but not all of them. Many priests have been strong supporters of the Solidarity Movement. And, of course, having a Polish Pope encourages them, too."

"So, if these churches are so full, why is it that in Prague the beautiful old churches are mainly used for musical performances?"

"Czechs, recently, were not that religious. Maybe it was because they had different religions forced upon them by conquering governments, like the Austrian Hapsburgs."

As we neared the seaport, I recalled seeing TV reports of government clashes with Solidarity Movement demonstrators in Gdansk. There were images of well-shielded army units bashing the Solidarity demonstrators and the army's tank-mounted water cannons spraying demonstrators to the ground. But I didn't expect we'd see any of that in the seaport of Szczecin, where we were headed, though it was not too far from Gdansk.

Cousin Stas had asked us to telephone him when we got near Szczecin, so that he could guide us to their apartment. Stas was a sea captain, whom we'd met when he docked in New York City, some years before. The plan was to stay overnight at his apartment and then drive to a Stankievich family reunion the next day. Walter looked forward to meeting his father's sister, Aunt Ewa, who was now in her 90s.

As we turned a corner in the city, my heart leaped in my chest. Walter jammed on the brakes. Directly in front of us was a large armored tank blocking our way. On top of the tank, I saw a water cannon swiveling in different directions, as if looking for something to shoot at.

"Oh, my God," I shouted. "Walter, turn around quickly. Hurry up!"

Walter did so, as quickly as a motor home can on a narrow street. His face was flushed with stress.

"I guess we better look for a telephone on another street," I said, laughing nervously, as I loosened my grip on the door handle.

Finally, we got in touch with Stas, and he came out to lead us in. We were relieved to see his lanky frame and droopy-mustached face. Now, I thought, at least someone friendly knows we're here.

Stas's Polish wife, Miroslawa, greeted us at their apartment door with a warm *"Dzien Dobry"* (good day), and then she continued with mixed Belarusian and Polish conversation, in which Walter participated. Stas spoke some English and drew me into the conversation at times. Their teen-aged children, Marcin and Magda, who also spoke a little English, though shyly at first, seemed intrigued by the first Americans they'd ever met, and began asking many questions about life in America. "Where do you live? Do you have a house of your own? Do you have children? Where are they?" Their questions started a flow of relaxed conversation, as we got to know more about each other.

We stayed overnight in their living room. After everyone went to bed, I enjoyed looking at the many artifacts from different ports in the world where Stas had traveled: Alaska, Iceland, and other locations around the North Atlantic.

The next morning, we followed Stas's car to meet the relatives in Czaplinek. Cousin Jozefa greeted us joyously at the gate to her farmhouse. She had the familiar, beaming, round Slavic face, like most of the Stankievich family.

Their farmland was separate from the house, on the outskirts of town. But as we walked around back, I could see that this was a true farmhouse. Several unpainted wooden shacks stood around a farmyard, with rust-colored chickens scratching the hard earth.

We walked up several steps to the kitchen door and, once inside, I noticed pans and dishes cluttering a small worktop and wood burning stove. A big meal was in preparation; I imagined that the chicken for dinner had just been plucked from their back yard.

The long table that filled the living room was obviously the gathering place for Jozefa's large family, all of whom were from the surrounding area. The table was laden with homemade condiments, including pickled mushrooms, beets, and salads, as well as various cold cuts. A half-drawn curtain revealed a back room: the sitting room-bedroom, which included a sofa and bed.

Someone brought Walter's aging Aunt Ewa from her apartment nearby. She was frail and quiet and wrapped in black clothing and a kerchief. To Walter's disappointment, she wasn't very communicative. Gradually, the rest of the family arrived. Besides Stas and his family, there was Josefa's husband and her brother, Jozef; Stas's sister, Irena, who was a mathematics professor, and her three children; and also Ewa's daughter, Zosia, and her husband, a local Communist official. The one major family member missing was Stefan, a high-ranking Polish naval officer.

Of all the relatives, I really enjoyed Jozefa's vitality most. After her initial shyness, she was outgoing and affectionate and hugged us in her ample arms. She bustled about the farm kitchen and seemed to be the center of the family configuration. Walter was laughing and talkative, obviously very happy to be meeting a part of his family whom he'd only heard about.

Later in the afternoon, I sensed a bit of tension. I looked up in alarm when a loud argument erupted between Jozef and Zosia's husband. A chair was slammed on the floor; someone fell against the wall. Walter was out in the yard at the time, so we never knew exactly what was said. But later, I learned that it was a political argument. The older Stankievich generation remembered their ill treatment by the Soviets all too well. After all, some of their relatives had been sent to labor camps in Siberia. Obviously, their different perspective from the Communist official was a strong point of contention between the families.

The younger professional members of the family did not participate in the discussion. Quite likely their work positions could have been jeopardized if they were reported making negative comments toward the government, whereas the farmers didn't feel as inhibited. My impression was that, in Poland during the summer of 1989, it was not quite so dangerous to express opinions that were anti-Soviet, as it was in Czechoslovakia.

Meeting these everyday people living under Communist rule, and seeing their varied responses to the regime, I found myself beginning to understand how difficult it was for them to keep their Belarusian national identity alive, here in Poland. Minorities, in general, were not given much latitude. Overall, it gave me a deeper appreciation of Walter's strong commitment to his national heritage, as well as being a patriotic American.

Later that evening in the motor home, I quizzed Walter about his impressions of our meeting with his relatives.

"It was good to be speaking Belarusian with them," he said, "though their speech is now, understandably, mixed with Polish words. The Belarusian atmosphere – sitting around a long table, with farm goodies like pickled wild mushrooms – was certainly familiar from my Belarusian experiences in the United States. And I really enjoyed getting all the family histories straight."

"Yes, it must be exciting to meet your father's relatives," I said.

"But, you know, Joanne, Father didn't even know most of them. He left the farm for school, and sometimes it wasn't safe to return, because of shifting borders. Then the war intervened. These people were strangers to me as well, unlike my Czech relatives, with whom I'd lived."

I admired the fortitude that these relatives had shown in making the best of poor circumstances; eventually, they'd left Belarus for an uncertain life in Poland. Certainly, the older generation in Czaplinek had kept their Belarusian language and culture, even if the younger generation had integrated more into their new life in Poland – actually, quite normally true for any second generation.

Though the first immigrating families continued to farm in Poland, they made sure their children received a good education, in order to have better opportunities. From the leadership positions a number of the younger generation held, I could see that the family was of intelligent, hardy stock, and I concluded: I married well.

Typical Belarusian village house

10
HARASSED BY COMMUNIST POLICE

After our quieter interlude with the Czaplinek relatives, we drove to Warsaw to meet with some local students and a New York area dance group, who were flying in to perform at a Belarusian Folk Festival in Bialystok. It was the first major Belarusian festival permitted since the Communists had taken power.

At the Student Center, I was introduced to some of the local leaders: Valik, Yolanta, Mirek, and Basia. They were dashing around, trying to get more fliers run off to advertise the event. I wondered if they would be the future leaders of a Belarusian movement in the eastern part of Poland, where so many Belarusians lived. Of course, the other possibility was that their activism might be persecuted, if the hoped-for freedoms were squelched again.

At the airport, Alla, a close friend from our dating days in the late 1950s, was first off the plane. She waved at us as she disembarked, her red hair making her stand out from the others. As Director of the dance group, she had arranged their performance at the Bialystok festival with the help of Piotr, a local who had become acquainted with this group while working in the United States.

"Oh, my God, can you imagine what it was like to get off the plane and look up at the airport balcony to see the Belarusian flag of independence being held by the students?" Alla said, with tears in her eyes, at her first sight of Eastern Europe since the war. She gave us the traditional Belarusian three-kiss greeting and said, "Hey, I haven't seen you two since you moved to Europe last year. What have you been doing?"

We told her about visiting Walter's relatives in Prague and being followed by the police there. Then, I shared with her the story of our encounter with the water cannons on the streets of Szczecin.

"Oh, my goodness, I wonder what our group being here might stir up?" she said. I wondered, too.

While the dance group practiced the next day, Piotr arranged for several of us to tour Belavezha (spelled Bialowieza on Polish maps). Belavezha is a national historic park, a part of the World Heritage primeval forest, spanning the Poland-Belarus border.

As Walter and I drove south to the forest, the environs changed considerably. In Bialystok, we had primarily seen one- and two-story cinder block homes, most in need of paint. Just a few miles south of Bialystok, I suddenly felt as if I'd been transported back 100 years. Now, all we saw along the local dirt roads were small, unpainted clapboard houses, many with thatched roofs. Rickety wooden fences enclosed small yards. In the villages, some of the houses included painted, geometrically-carved decorations along the roof line and windows. The farmhouses were more utilitarian and often had a huge stork nest on one corner.

I noticed that there were hardly any cars. Instead, we saw many wooden carts, drawn by a horse with a yoke. Walter gave me a lesson in local lore:

"You can tell which yokes are Belarusian and which are Polish: the Polish yokes are leather; the Belarusian yokes are those graceful, high-reaching, wooden ones." He pointed to one passing, and the farmer waved back.

I asked him why we didn't see any tractors in this area of Poland.

He said, "That's an indication that the Polish government doesn't invest as much money in the Belarusian region of the country." I was beginning to feel the strains of a Belarusian population being ruled by another government. It had also been evidenced in town signs, with crossed-out Polish words, and the insertion of the Belarusian spelling, such as Hajnauka for Hajnowka.

We gave a ride to a trudging farm lady, and she invited us into her farmhouse. We stepped into a large kitchen with a tiled wood-burning stove. The stove provided not only heat and a cooking area, but also an area at the back where, during cold winter nights, a pallet could be placed for sleeping. Open shelves above a sink held dishes and pans; curtains covered whatever was below the sink. In the center of the room was a long wooden table, with four simple chairs. Off to the side was another room. It seemed to be a sitting-bedroom area, partly hidden by a hanging blanket used as a curtain – similar to Jozefa's farmhouse in Czaplinek.

We were embarrassed by the woman's insistence on sharing a meal of sausage and pickled mushrooms with us: I was concerned that it might deplete her presumably small larder of food. But she seemed excited to be hosting Walter, a Belarusian from America, who worked for Radio Free Europe/Radio Liberty. And I was delighted to have this spontaneous insight into local life.

Finally, we arrived outside the small village of Belavezha. We were met by Piotr and a guide, as well as three other people who joined the group.

I was intrigued by the sight of a *zubr*, a gentle, bison-like animal that lives in the forest, rather than on the plains. As we went deeper into the forest, the guide pointed out an oak tree that had stood since the early 14ᵗʰ century. I was awestruck to think of all the chaotic man-made history that had occurred during its lifetime, while it remained standing in one place!

One man in the group seemed never to look at us, but always stood very close, which indicated to me that he was the informer in the group. But, after Walter's dismissal of my previous observations, I wasn't going to say a word.

As we walked along, Walter was talking very freely with Piotr about Belarusian affairs. At one point, Piotr turned his back to the others, motioned for silence with a finger to his lips, and whispered, "This man is known to us." He was nodding his head in the direction of the person I'd already identified. Walter understood that we should not talk so freely in his presence. The man was evidently assigned to us, since we saw him walking near us several more times during our two visits to Belavezha.

The Belarus Folk Festival was held that first weekend in a large outdoor amphitheater in Bialystok. Seating was slanted on a hillside, toward a stage decorated with typical Belarusian red and white colors. At the side of the stage hung the traditional white-red-white striped Belarusian flag of independence, not the current Soviet-inspired Belarusian flag. We were seated on one side, so we could see most of the audience. As I looked at the group, something puzzled me. I turned to Walter.

"Why do people keep pointing to the stage?"

"Well," he whispered, as his eyes swept around us, "since that flag has never been allowed to be displayed at a public event in Communist Poland before, people are afraid the police will go on stage and take it down. After all, it's neither the Polish flag, nor the current Soviet BSSR flag. It represents a Belarus nation, independent of outside control." Now, I understood the defiance it stated, and the danger of displaying it.

Admittedly, my watching the performances was distracted by this concern, as I kept looking from the performers to the police and audience. Thankfully, the police decided not to remove the flag. Talking to people later, I learned that the continued flying of the flag that day had brought real hope that this might be the dawning of a Belarusian minority movement in Poland.

Although distracted by the flag situation, I tried to focus back at the performers onstage, and I saw that the costumes were more varied than ones I'd seen at Belarusian events in New Jersey. Most of the men wore white costumes with wide pants, a tunic, and an embroidered sash at the waist. Women wore puffy-sleeved white blouses and colorful, long full skirts. The skirts were covered with white aprons that had embroidered red geometric designs edged along the bottom or sides. Some women also wore long embroidered streamers hanging from their hair.

The performances included several choral groups, some individual singers, a local band, and different dance groups. Much of the music was wistful, transporting my thoughts into the midst of waving wheat fields.

The mostly Belarusian audience – from both sides of the border – was enthusiastic and appreciative. However, also interspersed among the crowd were police, informers, and planted hecklers. Evidently, although the event was sanctioned, some authorities hadn't agreed with that decision. Even before the American group began to perform, several people booed their presence, which only encouraged louder clapping by the rest of the audience.

After the performance, as we talked with the American dance group, they told us that they'd been harassed since their arrival a few days earlier, presumably with official approval.

"Somebody wrote anti-American graffiti on the building across from our hotel. There wasn't any graffiti there when we arrived, so I suppose it was done to make us feel unwelcome," one of the Americans said.

Another added, "During our practice time, someone went through my luggage. Nothing was stolen, but they tossed my clothing all over the floor. I guess they wanted us to know we were under surveillance."

Why do they do such things? I asked myself. What could the police fear from these young American teenagers? One could only conclude that, from the government's point of view, *any* contact of their population with Western thinking posed a threat to the government's stringent control.

Since this was the weekend of June 21st, a *Kupalle*, a Belarusian Summer Solstice ceremony, took place after the festival. Many of those planning the festival were invited to join the American group at the home of a local Belarusian who lived above a stream (the stream was needed for the ceremony). A pungent kielbasa-in-a-roll meal was served to those of us gathered in the yard. Then, as dusk approached, we all walked through the nearby meadow and down to the stream.

Some of the group still wore ethnic costumes from their festival performance. Many of the women had added wreaths to their hair. Before starting down the hill, we were each given a candle. As we carefully edged our way down the dark, narrow path to the stream, the group began softly singing Belarusian folk songs. The melodic music echoed out over the water. I looked at the stream: the moon's reflection seemed to ripple across the water in waves. It was a quiet, inspirational moment, soothing me and lifting my thoughts to a sense of oneness with the universe.

After the singing by the side of the stream, the wreaths were taken off the girls' heads. Several candles were lodged on each wreath, and then the wreaths were carefully placed in the water, to float peacefully away. Some of the wreaths bumped into others, while others sped ahead on a faster current. This ceremony was accompanied with the singing of "Kupalinka," a song dedicated to the pagan solstice deity, Kupala.

Walter had missed the ceremony. Early during the event, he grabbed my arm, leaning in to whisper, "I'm going to have to leave you here for awhile. Stick near the American group. You'll be alright."

"What? Where are you going?" My voice squeaked with alarm.

"There's an underground Belarusian Democratic Committee in the area. They want to talk about the changing political situation under Glasnost, and how we see it at the Radios." Later, I learned that they also strategized about gaining more rights in Poland and how they might help the BSSR (Byelorussian Soviet Socialist Republic) move toward greater freedom from Soviet control.

One by one, the local Belarusian leaders were summoned from the ceremony with a whisper, "It's time now." Then, they were led cautiously up a dark path to the house on the hill. As the leaders gradually disappeared, I saw various informers quickly darting here and there in the dark, trying to find where their "assignments" had gone, and I laughed to myself at their ineptitude.

At the end of the festival, at about 1 a.m., with many of the candles now gone, it was quite dark as we tried to find our way back up the path. I waited patiently by the cars with other wives and girlfriends, until the clandestine meeting finished around 2 a.m. I was shivering a bit, not sure if it was from the cold or from the sense of danger surrounding the meeting. After all, the local government might legitimately consider their discussions reason for imprisonment. I could only hope that the meeting had not been infiltrated by an informer. Though Walter's sharing with them was for the purpose of advancing the cause of Belarusian freedom, if discovered, it could also end in abridging them.

Finally, the group from the meeting straggled back – Walter being almost the last to arrive – and we were safely on our way.

I was beginning to understand the paranoia people felt about the ever-present informers. To be informed on could mean losing your job, being sentenced to jail, or worse. And, of course, some of the charges might be trumped up, such as if someone wanted to "get ahead," or smear someone they didn't like. On the other hand, many informers were forced to spy on others because someone in authority was blackmailing them. It's "rule by fear," I concluded, and thought, How awful that generations of children have grown up in this environment.

Belarusian-American dance group

11
BUGGED IN BELAVEZHA

I felt I was handling the annoyances of informers well, with only a shrug or a comment. But the harassment escalated and finally rattled me. One day we were to meet the dance group for an outdoor performance in the town of Belavezha, at a small, end-of-the-line railroad station.

The motel the group was staying in was geared to attract Eastern bloc tourists visiting the Belavezha primeval forest. My first impression of the motel wasn't positive: it was a run-down, three-story, wooden structure in an industrial section of town. We'd decided to stay in the motel as a break from sleeping in the motor home, which we left in the motel's side parking lot.

As we entered the motel foyer, I cringed at the sight of sparse, blond, plasticized furniture, sitting on cracked linoleum. Our room wasn't much better, containing only a bed and a nightstand with one leg so short that it wobbled each time I touched it. The windows didn't work well, and the hard thin mattress was not inviting. As I surveyed the room, I began to think we'd made a mistake by not staying in the motor home. We were tired, though, because of the late meeting the previous night, so we set our bags down, changed, stretched out, and soon fell asleep.

At 4 a.m. I awoke, feeling that something was very wrong, and I needed to act on my intuition. (I call my intuitions "Angel Messages". Heeding them had protected us from danger several times.)

I tried to rouse Walter, shaking him and talking quietly,

"Walter, I think we need to go out and check the motor home."

"I'm not getting up in the dark to go outside. Check it yourself, if you want to." He turned away and went back to sleep.

I sat up in bed for a few minutes. I was hesitant to go by myself, although dawn was starting to lighten the sky. Okay, so he doesn't want to go out, I thought, but something is definitely wrong. If I put my coat on over my nightgown, I can go out and check, and then go back to sleep in the motor home.

As I walked out the front door, I was surprised to see a man smoking a cigarette at the far end of the motel. My suspicions grew, as I rounded the corner to where the motor home was parked. The motor home door was open! Looking in, I could see that food, papers, and clothing were strewn about on the floor. For a moment, I stood there in shock. I closed the door and dashed back inside the motel.

"Walter, wake up! Someone broke into the motor home!" This time I was shouting at him.

"What?" This news woke him up fast. He put on his clothes, while I quickly changed. Then we both rushed to the motor home to check the damage. Not much seemed to be missing, except for a box of cocoa and some vitamins. Someone had used the toilet and had not bothered flushing it – which seemed strange. It reminded me of an animal purposely violating another's territory to signal its dominance.

"We'll have to report the break-in to the police," Walter said.

"I don't know, I have a feeling it might have been the police who did this. I think that man I saw smoking at the side of the building was a lookout and alerted them to my coming." I thought if we'd gone out right away, when I sensed danger, we might have prevented the break-in, but it wasn't the time to mention that.

Pointing to a red car next to our motor home, Walter said, "Joanne, that can't be, this car has its door open, too, and must have been burglarized."

"I don't know, but in the last Ludlum spy novel I read the same thing happened. They broke into another car just to make it appear that the first one wasn't a police action. I'll bet they bugged our motor home."

"Oh, for heaven's sakes, stay here, while I go inside and make the call," Walter said. He was obviously upset with what he thought was my foolish thinking, let alone the burglary. But I was upset too and felt very vulnerable.

Two police cars and six policemen responded to Walter's telephone call. It seemed a bit of an overkill. They asked questions about why *we* were there and what *we* were doing.

Soon after, some of the dance group members started coming out of the motel and began asking what had happened. The local students, however, seemed to take this kind of harassment in stride and exchanged quiet, knowing looks. It was, after all, part of their daily life.

The police made a dramatic scene out of dusting the motor home for prints, but they didn't do much with the car next to ours. My suspicions may have been correct, after all, I thought.

A policeman told Walter that we would need to come down to the police station to be fingerprinted: that was the only way they could know which prints belonged to us and which belonged to the perpetrators.

My usually unflappable husband was beginning to see how dangerous the situation had become. Since the Polish government might consider Radios personnel to be CIA operatives, the police request for our fingerprints held ominous possibilities. Who knew what they might try to "prove", if they had our prints?

At that point, it was hard to know whether this was just a local police action against us, or a larger KGB move. (Later, a friend told us that the local police had indeed bugged our motor home "under orders.") At any rate, we'd had friends disappear in Soviet-controlled Eastern Europe – never to be heard from again – and we weren't taking any chances.

So, Walter replied in Polish to the police request, "We have to be someplace else in a few minutes." It was about 7 a.m. by then. "We'll come by the station later." They looked a little flustered, as clearly they weren't used to someone not immediately following their orders, but they gave us extra time to get to the police station.

We had previously arranged to visit Lonik, an artist friend of ours, that day, in a nearby village. We called and asked if we could come earlier. Then we packed up our belongings, paid our bill, and left the motel. We had no intention of either returning to that motel or of going to the police station to be fingerprinted. Not surprisingly, I noticed a police-type blue van traveling behind us on the road as we left the motel.

When we met Lonik, he sympathized with our predicament and suggested we stay in his compound for a couple of days. Lonik was considered a major Polish artist, though he was actually of Belarusian heritage. With hard currency earned from selling his paintings, he had been allowed to purchase an abandoned schoolhouse to use as an art studio and living quarters. He'd enclosed the yard with a high wooden fence and added a number of sheds that housed carrier pigeons and many exotic birds, his special interest.

I was relieved that in this compound we would be removed from prying eyes. I had to admit, with the morning's events, tension was overwhelming me. But Lonik was giving us a private hideout, and I intended to use it to recover my equanimity.

I was grateful for the distraction when Lonik showed us his paintings. Many were floor-to-ceiling black and white paintings, echoing the Belarusian countryside, in what appeared to be row upon row of birch trees or cart tracks in the snow. In his workroom – evidently the previous classroom – layers of paint littered the floor, without any attempt at clean-up, most likely considered a painter's haven.

I knew I had to face my fears, though, not just be distracted from them. As Walter spent the evening with local Belarusian leaders, I retired to the motor home parked in the enclosed yard. I wanted some quiet time. I needed to come back to the assurance that God was protecting us, no matter where we were.

I read some Psalms, while thinking, My location is always in "the secret place of the Most High." I prayed to feel God's presence and power surrounding us. I started the car and played a favorite cassette tape, "Peace and Joy and Power". My sense of freedom and joy returned.

Walter and I were both exhausted from the day's events, and we slept well that night.

The next day started out sunny, with the oppressive burden lifted. I felt fortified to combat whatever nonsense the police might try. I was determined: No matter what, I'm not going to let them take away my rediscovered joy.

That day we attended the outdoor Belarusian folk festival and another Solstice celebration.

The performances took place on the slightly raised train platform, with a large audience standing around ogling the performers above others' shoulders. Besides the featured American dance group, the other performing groups were more local and folksy, and not as professional as those in Bialystok.

As we watched the performances, I pointed out to Walter the man and his son who I'd previously thought had been assigned to listen in on us during our visit to the Belavezha Forest. By now, even Walter admitted that he was monitoring us. Oh, for heaven's sake, I thought with exasperation. Do they think Walter's a spy, here to report back about the situation on the ground? (Admittedly, Walter was thoroughly debriefed upon his return to the Radios.)

During the event, our friend Valik sidled up to Walter and said, "Someone came across the border from Belarus to see you. Can you get away to meet him behind the platform building?"

Walter is short, so the informer, who was standing on the railroad station balcony for a better view, didn't see him meld into the crowd. Suddenly the watcher started looking left and right, trying to locate Walter. I just chuckled: Another point for us.

Evidently, the person Walter was meeting often came across the porous, wooded Belarus-Polish border at night, stayed for an hour or so, and then disappeared back. He'd heard that Walter would be at this event and wanted to confer about Radio Free Europe/Radio Liberty broadcasts. Later, Walter told me that they went off into the bushes to talk for a few minutes. Then the man left quickly, leaving Walter standing awkwardly alone in the bushes. Walter looked around to see the reason for the sudden departure, thinking maybe the person had become aware of someone observing them — or maybe it'd been a set-up. He came back to me with a quizzical look on his face, as if to say: I don't know what that was all about.

In contrast to the evening before, when he had missed the ceremony because of the clandestine meeting, this time Walter was able to attend and enjoy the Solstice ceremony following the festival. By now, some of the American young people were feeling quite comfortable with their Belarusian counterparts. After the laying of the wreaths, one of Alla's sons, and a couple of other young people, ended the evening by exuberantly jumping into the stream. I was glad that they had fun memories to take back to the States, and not just the harassment stories.

It was very late and dark as we traveled back to Lonik's compound. There were no other cars on the road, except some lights behind us. We mistakenly made a wrong turn into a dead end and had to make a U-turn back onto the street. Of course, the familiar blue van also had to make that same U-turn, finally convincing Walter, "I have to admit, that may be a police van following us."

As we drove along, with the menacing lights still behind us, it seemed like a good idea to lighten the mood. So, since I was convinced that the police had indeed bugged our motor home, I leaned over, speaking into the dashboard loudly, "Maybe we should tell them that those are just your vitamins they took. It could save them the bother of testing for drugs, with the hope of catching us on some charge." Walter laughed. Humor helped break the tension.

The next day, we were glad to be on our way home to Munich. I'd had enough of political intrigues, and of being constantly monitored and harassed. We hadn't had anything calamitous happen to us, yet I knew that several instances could have turned out disastrously, and I gave thanks for what I felt was protection "from on High."

Just before reaching the orderly calm of West Germany, we had one last tension-producing event at the border. The East German border guards, as we'd become accustomed to in Eastern Europe, gave special attention to our passports, taking them into a shed and delaying us more than others. One guard, with a hand on his gun, entered the motor home. He inspected every cabinet and lifted up seats, before leaving. Looking out the window, I motioned for Walter to come and see what was going on outside.

"Look. What are they doing with those things they're rolling under the motor home?"

"Those are mirrors on wheels. They're trying to make sure we're not smuggling someone under the motor home – someone desperate to leave their Socialist Heaven." I laughed again at their strange antics. But at the same time, I realized that desperate people were, indeed, sometimes smuggled out to the West in that manner.

Later that day, as we pulled in front of our Munich apartment, I rejoiced at the prosperity of life in Western Europe. I saw it with new appreciation: How wonderful to live in a democratic society without the constant fear of oppressive, arbitrary government action!

Something had changed in me. The late 1950s McCarthy-era tactic of using Americanisms to hound often innocent people out of jobs had jaded my view of American symbols. That week, as I saw the American flag waving over the Radios building, I felt a surge of patriotism and renewed appreciation for all the good it stood for.

Steve, hacking his piece of the Berlin Wall

12
A NEW WORLD ORDER EMERGES

That 1989 summer trip behind the Iron Curtain had directly reinforced my view of the Soviet empire as having devastated the people and countries of Eastern Europe. This was evidenced in the padded doors, the spying house informers, the necessarily circumspect conversations, long lines for basic foods, rundown buildings, and shabbily dressed, unsmiling people. Two generations had been brought up in fear of the knock on the door that could arbitrarily change one's life. To the outside world, the Soviet grip on power in Eastern Europe appeared indestructible.

The political struggle between East (the Soviet Union and the countries under its control) and West (the United States and Western Europe) had dominated my whole adulthood. Fear of nuclear war was a constant concern for many people, especially during the 1962 Cuban missile crisis, when it seemed that either Khrushchev or Kennedy might press the red button and create a nuclear holocaust. Some Americans had built underground bomb shelters, in anticipation of that day. We knew that the Soviet Union had a large enough nuclear stockpile to obliterate most Western cities, and the long-range missiles to deliver them. All of American foreign policy was geared toward containing that threat. No one wanted a Third World War. But how else could the Cold War end?

Soon after we settled back into life in Munich, I asked Walter, "What do you think is the possibility of your relatives in the East gaining Western-style freedoms any time soon?"

He answered that it didn't seem likely. "The Soviets won't want to give up their hegemony over Eastern Europe. It's what makes them a world power."

"I know, but I heard recently that Yugoslavia and Hungary have allowed some economic reforms, with private enterprise," I said. "Doesn't that indicate change might be coming?" Hungary had even taken down its barbed wire fencing at its border with Austria, in a bid to attract Western investments.

"It's true that some of those outer-edge countries in the Soviet Bloc have gotten away with a few reforms – at least for now," he replied. "But they're still Communists. And we've also seen the violent crackdowns on the Solidarity movement in Poland."

I understood Walter's strong anti-Communism stance, yet I wanted to have hope of change for those relatives I'd recently met and come to care about. From my positive-thinking standpoint, I viewed Glasnost, the opening of some borders, and impending talks between Solidarity and the Polish government as glimmers of hope.

These glimmers of hope had been lit on December 7, 1988, when Mikhail Gorbachev, then leader of the Soviet Union, announced, "Freedom of choice is a universal freedom," in speaking about the European satellite countries. His ideas for Glasnost and *Perestroika* (restructuring of the economic and political society) had already begun to percolate into actions. People in the West hailed his new policies for bringing more freedoms to the Soviet Union and countries under Soviet control. (As honored as he became in the West for this shift – even winning the 1990 Nobel Peace Prize – Gorbachev's popularity at home eventually plummeted, as the consequences of his ideas played out, and Soviet power disintegrated under his presidency.)

To our amazement, events in late 1989 catapulted countries of Eastern Europe into a new world order of freedom from Soviet tyranny. One after another of those countries gained freedom from Communist rule. It was hard for my mind to adjust to the swiftness of it. I couldn't have imagined, even in my wildest hopes, that such changes could happen – and with almost no violence.

Walter kept saying, in amazement at the unfolding events, "I came to the Radios at the perfect time!" It was exhilarating for him to be in the middle of hearing about, and reporting on, these history-making events. Every night, I eagerly quizzed him, "Tell me the latest news," knowing that he had inside information being fed directly to the Radios from underground stringers inside the satellite countries. It was fascinating for me to hear Walter's side of the news, which greatly augmented the short English-language BBC and Sky News TV stories we listened to from Great Britain.

The first surprising event came in August of 1989. Walter came home with the news: "Joanne, the Polish government promises free parliamentary elections." But he added, with skepticism, "We'll see how 'free' they really are." Solidarity advocates had gained greater power during the summer, aligning themselves not only with workers, but also with students and intellectuals. The Polish government hadn't been able to contain the increasing political unrest with martial law and felt forced to move forward with elections. The Communists were stunned by their sound defeat. By the fall, presidential elections were called for, and Lech Walesa, the electrician who was head of the Solidarity dockworkers union, was elected President of Poland.

I rejoiced for Cousins Stas and Jozefa and their families in Poland: new possibilities would now be open to them!

Walter alerted me to another development. For East Germans, the crack in the Iron Curtain significantly widened in August of 1989, when East German tourists began crossing the border by the thousands, on a route through Czechoslovakia into a somewhat freer Hungary. From Hungary, they immigrated across the newly opened Hungarian border into neutral Austria and back up to West Germany. Camps were set up in Austria to support and sustain the travelers on their way. It continued to the point where West German resources were being strained by their entry.

"Surely, the Soviet Union won't allow this kind of mass exodus – whatever Gorbachev's stated policies," I said to Walter. We were both bracing for the expected reaction. We presumed that the Soviets would probably crack down on this migration to the West with the use of troops, just as they did in Hungary in 1956 and in Czechoslovakia in 1968. The pattern seemed clear.

What most people didn't know, then, was that the internal economic strain on the Soviet Union to keep up the arms race with the West had stretched the Soviets almost to the limit. Some later reports indicated that the promised billions in aid from the West – to cover a grain shortfall – was so crucial to averting famine, at that point, that the Soviet Union could not risk its possible withdrawal if they cracked down militarily in Eastern Europe. They were also already militarily overextended and simply didn't have enough troops and materiel to successfully quell rising unrest in a number of satellite countries at once. And that seemed the stage events had reached, with both Polish and German unrest roiling to the surface.

Added to that situation, some of the old hard-line Communist politicians were dying off, along with their ideology. Gorbachev's newer policies contributed to the political confusion. Communist leaders in Eastern Europe were no longer certain of receiving military back-up if needed in a crackdown, so they hesitated to act when faced with opposition. That hesitation gave fuel to the opposition.

In October, 70,000 East Germans, encouraged by church leaders, marched silently along the streets of Leipzig, holding lighted candles to protest for a peaceful resolution of the volatile situation in East Germany. To the astonishment of many, almost not a shot was fired, as candle demonstrations increased throughout repressive East Germany.

"Turn the TV on, Joanne, they're breaching the Wall!" Walter called from work with that news on November 10, 1989.

"Are you sure?" I asked in amazement. The Berlin Wall – a barrier constructed of concrete, barbed wire, guard towers, and crossing checkpoints – had stanched the previously easy flow of East German defectors to the West since August of 1961. It stood through John F. Kennedy's 1963 heralded "Ich bin ein Berliner" (I am a Berliner) speech and Ronald Reagan's 1987 rally: "Mr. Gorbachev, tear down this wall!" Over the years, hundreds had been killed and wounded trying to tunnel under or cross it. That wall had symbolized Soviet repression. If it was coming down, then one could only assume that it prefigured the end of Soviet control in Eastern Europe.

Later, Walter shared rumors that the fall of the Berlin Wall had actually hinged on a mistake. There had been a change in the

East German government, and the new *Politburo* (the chief policy-making body) voted to meet some of the demands of the people for freer access to the West – not in any way expecting it to mean the end of Communist control in East Germany. The results of the meeting were announced on TV by Gunter Schabowski, a spokesman for the Politburo. While reporting, he was asked *when* free access to the West would come into effect. He hesitated, not sure, then said, essentially, "Now."

Listeners to the program were stunned. Many East Berliners started for the Wall, to test if the report was really true. Some checkpoints rejected them, not having had any directives about such actions. But other guards had heard the program, and they ushered them through into West Berlin – some even removed barriers, to facilitate a faster exit. Soon, people climbed up on top of the Berlin Wall, tearing down the barbed wire, and dancing; then others began chopping away at the concrete wall.

One East German man wandered onto Kurfurstendam, the main West Berlin shopping street. He was awed at the abundance of everything in the stores, though he didn't have money to buy anything. "No wonder they didn't allow us to cross over the wall. We'd have seen the vast difference with our empty stores." He noticed that people on the streets smiled, and looked prosperous, in contrast to the dreary endurance people in the East exhibited.

Many people crossing over the Wall dashed immediately to the door of a relative, whose home they hadn't been allowed to visit since 1962, though it may have been only a mile or so from their own. It was a time of great rejoicing, the world over!

The fall of the Berlin Wall started an avalanche. I watched on BBC as unrest escalated in Czechoslovakia after a November 17th police attack on student demonstrators. Rumors spread that a student was killed, though this was later refuted. But the rumor galvanized the rest of the Czech population: millions joined in a general strike, and 100,000 demonstrators flowed down Jindriska Street toward Wenceslas Square. They held signs – *"Svoboda"* (freedom) and *"Demisi"* (resign) – directed at the Communist government. The police now refused to fire on their fellow citizens, and the Velvet Revolution, as it was later called, began.

Walter closely followed what was happening in Czechoslovakia, since he was familiar with some of the players and knew Czech Radios broadcasters well. A loose group of intellectuals, most of them signatories of the Czech Charter 77 Human Rights Manifesto, organized a group called the Civic Forum, to begin formulating policies for a hoped-for new government. They didn't want a softer Communist government, but rather an independent democracy. By the end of November, the now almost-defunct Czechoslovak Communist government agreed that free elections would be held.

In early December, Vaclav Havel, the quiet, unassuming playwright, recently released from prison, agreed to become President of an interim government. Alexander Dubcek, the former leader of the 1968 Prague Spring, was brought back as the Speaker of the Parliament. That transition would take a new turn later, as the country quietly split into separate Czech and Slovak Republics in 1993.

Within about a year's time, all the countries considered European Soviet satellites gained their independence. For Walter, one question remained: What would become of the federation of Republics in the Soviet Union itself, including Walter's homeland of Belarus? Could they also spin out of Soviet control? In 1990, that still didn't seem likely to most people I spoke with – but then, who could have predicted the changes in Eastern Europe?

Spontaneous expressions of new-found freedom

13
CHRISTMAS AMIDST THE VELVET REVOLUTION

By Christmas of 1989, when we traveled back to Prague, the Velvet Revolution was not yet totally secure. It wasn't until December 29 that Vaclav Havel was installed as President of a democratic Czechoslovakia.

Before meeting Walter's relatives at the lake for Christmas festivities, we wanted to get the flavor of what was still taking place in Prague, so we stopped at Wenceslas Square. Even though it was many days after the larger demonstrations – which reached half a million people – crowds still reverently surrounded the improvised shrine to Jan Palach, a young Czech who had immolated himself in an earlier protest. Hundreds of candles and flowers lay at the foot of the statue of St. Wenceslas; many were in front of small photos of individuals who had perished during Communist rule. Some people waved Czech red-blue-white flags.

People gathered joyfully and tearfully. Some hugged anyone passing by, in a show of togetherness. There was an evident emotional energy, not seen on our last trip; it was like pent-up hope, suddenly released. The crowd was mostly younger; after all, the demonstrations had started with students just a few weeks earlier, on November 17.

Older residents had at first been reluctant to participate. They remembered all too well the crackdown after the freer period of the Prague Spring, in 1968. Some of these older Czechs still seemed incredulous, not certain if the promised freedoms would really last. Soviet troops were still on Czech soil, though now kept in their barracks.

As we walked the length of Wenceslas Square, I saw store windows plastered with slogan posters. There were many: "Svoboda" (freedom), "Havel na Hrad" (Havel to the castle), or others showing sly Czech irony such as, "Teacher, you don't have to lie to us anymore."

"Havel to the Castle" intrigued me. At that time, Vaclav Havel had already been nominated by the Civic Forum to fill the interim post of President of Czechoslovakia. Although not a politician, Havel's power was in the steadfast moral courage he'd shown in his opposition to the Communists throughout their rule of Czechoslovakia. Most of his extensive and outspoken writings had only been available to Czechs as *Samizdat* (underground) material, passed from one hand to another. As a major promoter of the Charter 77 Manifesto for Human Rights, he helped draw important signatories, whose names were then broadcast over the Czech Service of RFE/RL. Havel was revered by the population for his continuing voice of decency, in a world where most feared the consequences.

Under the dark arches on Narodni Trida, the street where the riots had taken place, we saw another memorial of lit candles and wreaths of flowers. It was where the student had been reported killed. I sensed a quieter reverence in the smaller crowd gathered there.

I could hardly believe it: we were right there, in the midst of Czechoslovakia's Velvet Revolution!

With the backdrop of seeing these exciting changes, we met our Czech relatives for a memorable Christmas together at the lakeside cottage, outside the village of Vyzlovka. Now we could speak freely with them, and some revelations came forth.

Mirek told us, "Helenka and I sometimes listened to Radio Free Europe." I looked over at his daughter, Andulka. Her eyes widened with disbelief, "You did?" she exclaimed. Obviously, if the children had known, and unwittingly blurted it out, it would have been reported, with possibly dangerous consequences. So, the listening had to be very secretive.

Mirek admitted quietly, just to me, "Since any contact with foreigners had to be reported, we did get quizzed by the police about our conversations with you last summer. We're so glad that's all past, now." Evidently, each government employee (and most everyone worked for the government) was required to report what was said in conversations with foreigners. Then, the authorities compared notes to see if it was accurately stated by each one, playing off the fear that one person's story might deviate from the other.

Cousin Helenka confided, "When Mirek sometimes traveled out of the country, I didn't want to go with him. I just didn't want to see the stark difference between our life here and life in the West."

On the day of Christmas Eve, the whole family bundled up warmly to walk through the woods to pick out a tree. It was a crisp, winter day. At first, we chatted along the route, with three-year-old Petia running ahead, pointing at squirrels and birds. As we strolled further into the leaf and needle-strewn pathway, the quiet of the forest prevailed, and we talked less and more quietly. Mirek commanded the scene, as he marched ahead and inspected different trees. Finally, he called back to us to check one out. It was a much scrawnier evergreen tree than we'd use in the States. This was of necessity, since the decorations would include real, lighted candles. When all agreed to use that tree, Mirek axed it down, and we hauled it back to the house. By then, we were glad to be back in the living room, with the cozy warmth of the wood-burning stove.

Aunt Anichka and Cousin Helenka puttered in the small, simple kitchen, preparing the Christmas Eve meal, which featured garlic soup and carp.

"This is a tradition," Mirek explained to me. "We buy the carp and keep them alive, swimming in the bathtub, until Christmas Eve." I recalled that, a day earlier, we had seen tubs filled with live fish on many Prague street corners. The carp was lightly floured, fried, and very tasty, though it left that fishy fragrance hanging in the air for the rest of the evening. I was hesitant about eating a soup made of garlic; but it turned out to be deliciously smooth, with a potato base. We'd brought a bag of oranges, as part of our contribution to the gathering. Since oranges could still not be bought locally, they were shared sparingly, a few pieces at a time.

Andulka led little Petia upstairs for awhile during the decorating of the tree. His eyes shone in wonder when he was called back in to see the candle-lit tree, with colorful home-made decorations and gifts under it. "From the baby Jesus," he was told. It had been a long time since we had savored a small child's Christmas awe – since our boys were now grown – and it made this Christmas even more special for us.

I thought, then, of our sons, John and Steve. Being separated at Christmas was hard. Surely, I thought, all the other young people in their shared college house will have gone home for Christmas. I hoped they were not sitting alone, having pizza or something; they'd told us that their Thanksgiving had been spent that way. I felt guilty that we couldn't afford a trip back to the States for Christmas; our Mountain Lakes house still hadn't been sold. But then I put those thoughts aside, to focus on enjoying this somewhat old-fashioned, European Christmas.

We sat around the long living room table on the built-in benches during the gift opening. Some of the gifts were simple: a bar of soap, a scarf, a toy for Petia. They were carefully unwrapped, the paper being folded for use the next Christmas. I forget which gift it was they gave us that year, but it was the start of their giving us special items, such as a samovar or an icon that had been left behind by Walter's parents, after their quick departure from Prague in 1945. I was very touched by this gesture of returning Walter's heritage to him.

After the gift-opening, Walter heartily joined in singing some of the Czech carols that he remembered from his childhood. Aunt Anichka's eyes glistened as she watched her sister's son, Walter, singing with her family. I felt a much stronger sense of unhindered family warmth now, as compared to our first meeting, when caution and uncertainty were ever-present. By the end of the evening, several eyes held tears: with gratitude for being together, with the hope of new and better times coming, and just for being able to celebrate Christmas openly again.

Late in the evening, the adults went to the Catholic Church in nearby Kostelec to attend the Midnight Mass. Although I didn't think our relatives were particularly religious, this was a special event. It was the first open Christmas church celebration since the

Communist takeover. The small church, with the centered cross holding a crucified Jesus, was filled with people rejoicing for this gift of unhindered religious expression.

What a joyous contrast this Prague trip was, compared to just six months before!

Director of Belarus Service, at RFE/RL Anniversary

14

SEARCHING FOR A NEW IDENTITY

The sudden shift in the political framework of Europe brought much upheaval – to countries as well as their people – as they struggled with the changing reality and establishing a new identity.

Exactly how can such a wrenching change take place: from total autocratic control to an open-society democracy and from a government economy to a capitalistic one? Not only did governments and economies have to be totally revamped, but individual thinking had to shift from entrenched fear and distrust toward more openness and creative thinking. Questions abounded, though answers seemed slow to appear.

As the East-West power struggle that had so dominated U.S. foreign policy receded, the United States was acknowledged as the major world power, a position which came with new responsibilities.

What help would be needed by the evolving countries, and how would the U.S. distribute it? Would a new Marshall Plan be drawn up, as after the war? There was great concern that a reunited and strong Germany might dominate Europe, possibly posing problems for a third time in the century. Alliances had to adjust: Should NATO be dismantled, now that it was no longer needed as a foil against the Warsaw Pact? And what about the Soviet Union: Will it become a democracy, too, or will it be pulled back by some strong ruler? Are we now friend, or still foe?

During this political turmoil, Walter and I were also working out a new sense of identity. He was shifting from his old image of himself as an engineer, to being a strong journalistic contributor at Radio Free Europe/Radio Liberty.

Walter had first taken the available position as a reviewer of Radios' programming, but it wasn't his desired activity. So he was delighted when, after a few months at the Radios, he was offered a newly opened position as a broadcaster in the Belarus Service. He then wrote and broadcast programming every day into Belarus, becoming a known and appreciated voice to thousands of Belarusians.

Then, within our first two years in Munich, he was appointed Director of the Belarus Service. I thought he might make an even better Director than journalist. While building our business in the States, he'd acquired good leadership skills, and he seemed to have fewer ego needs than others in the Service. I knew he was good at focusing on goals and enabling others to perform well. I imagine he took on the role with some trepidation – perhaps about his own capabilities, but more likely regarding the situation in the Service, at that time.

The Directorship certainly put more pressure on Walter. He not only had greater responsibility for programming, but personnel issues often plagued him. He'd come home with complaints like,

"_____ isn't talking to _____ and I had to be the go-between today, in order to get the programming out on time." There were incessant rumors and accusations amongst the workers, such as "_____ is a spy for the Soviets; he should be ousted from the Service." (Of course, there was some basis for paranoia. Documents found after the fall of the Soviet Union proved that a former chief editor of the Russian Service, Oleg Tumanov, had been spying for the Soviets for many years, as well as Czechs like freelancer "Albort" and others.)

Up until that time, the Belarus Service was comprised mainly of Belarusian emigrants who had left Belarus after the war and settled in Germany. Since Walter had lived in the United States, he had been exposed to a more American mindset; thus he brought a fresh perspective to the Director's position. One of his goals was to bring in younger personnel with specialized skills. By the end of our five years in Munich, Walter had filled six of the eight Service positions with younger Belarusian nationals from the Diaspora in four countries, as well as from Belarus.

Walter became well respected at the Radios for his quiet, yet persistent following through on matters he felt were important. For instance, he had the audacity to question the Washington-based Board for International Broadcasting (now Broadcasting Board of Governors) on the issue of inequity in Service staffing between the Radio Liberty section of the combined Radios and the Radio Free Europe section. Radio Free Europe, which covered Eastern Europe, had three to four times the number of staff in each Service, as compared to Radio Liberty, which broadcast into the Soviet Republics.

Eventually, the decision makers in Washington approved more staff for Radio Liberty, including the Belarus Service. With the somewhat freer political atmosphere, Walter was able to increase the number of freelance stringers in Belarus, making the news sections of the programming more relevant.

With Walter's advancement, we were also eligible for a better apartment, and we found one in Bogenhausen, the very area in which I'd envisioned living when we were still back in New Jersey. The location was perfect, just three blocks to work for Walter and near an entrance to the Englischer Garten, still a favorite walking area. There was local shopping, just two blocks away at Kufsteiner Platz, with a grocery store, bakery, meat shop, cleaners, and flower shop – bringing flowers was essential when visiting anyone in Germany. And the counter people at the local deli, Feinkost Marks, always welcomed me with a smile, making me feel an accepted part of the community.

Our spacious, two-bedroom apartment was in a new brick building on Pienzenauerstrasse, a street with single family homes, as well as a few low, modern apartment buildings. It was a ground-floor unit, with a tulip garden outside the kitchen window and a secluded patio with hanging red geraniums. The huge refrigerator and outdoor grill allowed for a more American lifestyle, and we immediately began having cook-outs with church and Radios friends.

Even as Walter was making a satisfying impact with his work, and we were establishing a comfortable home in Munich, I was facing another dilemma. I now knew we'd be in Europe many more years. In the beginning, it had been acceptable to spend most of my time adjusting to a new lifestyle and traveling. But now that I faced more years ahead in Europe, I wanted to build deeper friendships and find some worthwhile activity. I wanted to fill in that blank slate that was created when I'd left my many previous roles behind in America.

There were several ways I'd expected to find meaningful contacts in Munich: with Germans at church, Belarusians, and other RFE/RL international personnel, and at the American military base, where we had limited access.

But, as my efforts progressed, I felt thwarted. I enjoyed getting together with Michael and Julie, friends from the nearby Christian Science church. However, Walter wasn't as comfortable with our deep spiritual discussions, since he'd become jaded about religion because of its political corruption in Eastern Europe. Since we came with a more American perspective, we also didn't quite fit into the existing Belarusian émigré social environment. And, though our G-14 rating allowed me access to the Women's Club on the McGraw Kaserne military base, we weren't really accepted in the military pecking order, either.

We connected with a German equivalent of our previous U.S. business, but Walter didn't want to use his Radios' contacts for business, and I didn't have good German contacts, so that was slow in starting up.

Some of these avenues did offer opportunities to contribute my talents usefully. For instance, with my church friend, Julie, I offered to do a two-hour image consultation, including color analysis. I'd been trained in California as an image consultant by Bernice Kentner, author of *Color Me a Season*. I first tested Julie to see if a warm or a cool foundation was best for her. Then, I draped her with different colored fabric to determine that she was a "vibrant spring", needing bright jewel colors to complement her dark hair. Afterwards, she several times exclaimed, "It's made such a difference. I've started buying more colorful clothing, now that I'm sure of the right colors." That comment generated an idea: Maybe image consulting is something special, taken from my American business training, which I can bring to women in Europe.

At the military Women's Club, I presented two programs: Image Consulting and a Setting Goals Seminar. Both were well received, but I didn't see much follow-up there.

Through the Women's Club, one friendship developed with a German, Marina, who had lived in America and did massage therapy on the military base. Our get-togethers outside of the base were always stimulating and culturally expanding for me. From her, I learned some of the typical German mores, such as the importance of protocol in relationships. For instance, the Germans use formal titles in introducing people: "Herr Professor," "Herr Ingeneur," or "Herr Doktor." But this formality also stifled closeness, it seemed to me. Once, Marina said she'd like to bring her good friend with her for tea to my house.

"What is the first name of your friend?" I asked, wanting to introduce her to several others coming.

"I don't know," she answered, "I always refer to her as Frau (her last name)" – although they'd been friends for over ten years! I realized something. Germans have two words for "you": one for intimate relationships and another more formal "you." From Marina's explanation about her friend, I ascertained that my relationship with Marina probably wasn't ever going to be on an American-style intimate basis.

Somehow, in Germany, I didn't feel I was fitting in. And that puzzled me, since my mother was of German background, and I'd identified closely with her. She was a hard worker, a perfectionist, and a strong-willed achiever. My mother also expected perfection from others, including her children: perfect grades, perfect stitches in sewing, perfect ballet performances. I'd tried to live up to her expectations. But somewhere along life's journey, I'd come to realize that this perfectionism was anxiety-producing and sometimes unnecessary. I'd often wasted precious time reworking speeches, until spontaneity was probably erased from them. I realized that part of my attraction to Walter was his knack of saying, "It's good enough," and moving on.

As I pondered this question about not fitting in, it suddenly dawned on me that I'd spent most of my life consciously trying to soften some of those strong Germanic qualities instilled in me by my mother. Now, I felt a yearning for something to offset that strict orderliness and formality, even for short periods of time.

Feeling frustrated in my efforts to find my right path in Europe, I prayed more diligently for inspiration. I thought of a favorite quote: "Love inspires, illumines, designates, and leads the way." (*Science and Health with Key to the Scriptures*, by Mary Baker Eddy, page 454). With a sense of calm sureness, the word "Italy" jumped into my mind.

There was good reason for that idea: I'd started some people in business in Florence and Rome the year before we decided to move to Europe. Then, during the first year in Europe, I'd made several forays into Italy relating to the business, making some progress, but also encountering large stumbling blocks. I thought, Although it's a distance from Munich, building a strong business in Italy might allow me to contribute my talents in an environment I enjoy. I intuitively sensed that Italy was the place where I should focus my efforts to create a satisfying new *Me*.

Nanny goat intimidating Jewell and Joanne

15
THE FARM-GIRL IMAGE FADES

At different times in my life — especially when feeling unsure of my position — I'd fall back on thinking of myself as a simple farm girl. The first 18 years of my life had been spent on a 25-acre dairy farm outside of Monroe, Washington, about 50 miles north of Seattle. I'd always thought that farm life was ideal for children: getting to know the characters of different animals, appreciating the beauty of majestic mountains and wild streams, having a collie to lick your face in sympathy, and snuggling a new-born kitten.

Yet, at a reunion of our 1952 Monroe High School graduating class, a comment jolted me and made me question if I'd ever really fit the typical farm girl mode, even when I lived on the farm. At the reunion, we'd just finished reliving the winning state basketball championship, when one of the now-graying players approached me with a question:

"How is it, Joanne, that most of us still live around this area, but you've gone off to New York and Europe (in the 1960s) and done such interesting things, like working with Eleanor Roosevelt?"

I didn't know how to answer the question. When we'd gone around the room, checking where people lived and what they were doing, I'd noted that most still resided not far from our hometown. They were living very productive lives: working, contributing to their communities, going on vacations, and raising families – with many photos of grandchildren proffered. But I couldn't quickly identify why I'd moved so far away and been involved in activities so different from what, in the 1950s, had been considered normal for women: working as a secretary, nurse, or teacher; then getting married to a local boy and having babies.

Thus, on our first trip back to the States, I decided to find the answer to that question: What were the factors that turned my life in such a different direction, far away from my farm heritage? We flew back to New Jersey, first, to see our sons and friends, but then we traveled on to the Pacific Northwest to visit my relatives and hometown of Monroe.

While on the plane toward Sea-Tac airport, I thought about the farm. After my father died, my brother, Bill, took over the farm's operation. He was now gone, but my sister-in-law, Bettie, still lived on the farm. Their older son, Russ, and his family live in another house on the property and raise beef cattle. Tears welled up in my eyes, as I thought, I'm so grateful that the farm is still in the family, and I can go back to my roots every once in awhile. For me, there was stability in that fact – especially since we'd often lived in rental apartments in different countries.

Walter and I rented a car at the airport and drove 50 miles north, to Monroe and the farm.

During my childhood, Monroe was a small town of 1,500 people, with Main and Lewis streets crossing and a few stores – the feed store being the most prosperous. Farming was the main activity in the Skykomish, Tualco, and Snohomish Valleys, going off in different directions from the town.

Now, with the extension of Highway 522 from Seattle running directly to town, Monroe had become essentially a Seattle suburb, grown to around 15,000 people, ten times the population when I lived there.

After we turned onto Highway 2, which goes over Stevens Pass into Eastern Washington, we passed several busy, small malls, before turning down a side street, toward the town center. Childhood memories became activated as we drove by familiar landmarks.

The old high school building brought to mind the large-figured Miss Wick, the English teacher who taught me to love words. Unfortunately, when I would come back to the farm and try to use them, saying something like, "What was the *denouement* of that story?" my brother would guffaw, and say, "Listen to Smarty Pants," in a dismissive way, as if to say, "What good will those big words do you?"

As we drove into the town center, I was shocked to see that it had turned into a backwater of the highway, with antique shops replacing vibrant retail stores.

The old firehouse was now the Monroe Historical Society. It was in the town library, on the second floor over that firehouse, where my imagination had been whetted for other places and adventures. I'd been enthralled to read how Ataturk had transformed the Ottoman Empire into a more Western-style Turkey. Then, I was transfixed to read about political figures, like corrupt Boss Tweed in New York City, and Eugene V. Debs and his Socialist theories. Transcendentalist writings appealed to me, especially Emerson's essays, such as "Self Reliance", which brought me even closer to my own religion. These stories were shaping my future interests.

As we drove farther along Main Street, I looked for the Monroe Bakery where I'd worked part-time after I turned sixteen. That work provided me with money to buy things usually beyond the means of a Depression-era farm girl. For instance, I'd seen an ad in a magazine and purchased a set of classical records and a set of books about great artists. I listened for the first time to Beethoven, though I wasn't sure I really liked it; I was used to polkas, schottisches, western ballads, and pop music. But I loved the vibrancy of Van Gogh's sunflowers, and I scotch-taped a reproduction of the painting to my bedroom wall. These things were not a familiar part of my upbringing but, by my teens, I was eager to learn about things considered cultural. Perhaps that was an outcome of my mother's dictum: "I want better things for my girls."

From early childhood, Mother took us to her home city of Seattle, for performances of the Ice Follies, the Ballet Russe de Monte Carlo, and other cultural activities. I loved the beauty and grace of ballet. I took many years of ballet lessons, practicing long hours at home, performing in carefully sewn tutus and other costumes my mother made, and visualizing myself as a famous ballerina – until I saw Maria Tallchief dance, and I realized I didn't have the tall, willowy physique to be a successful ballerina. Mother also bought my younger sister Jewell a violin, so that she could take music lessons.

I'm not sure where Mother scrounged the money for these activities, as we kids sometimes overheard arguments between our parents when it became hard to meet mortgage payments. But, being of a determined German background, Mother found a way to show us that there were other things in life than just what we experienced on the farm. However, finding a way to realize a different lifestyle wasn't clear, since the farthest I'd travelled was over Stevens Pass to the Wenatchee Valley to buy crates of apricots for canning.

In my junior year of high school, I applied for college at the University of Washington; I thought that I might major in journalism and travel to school from the farm. With my mother's encouragement, I also applied to Principia College, an expensive private college for Christian Scientists, near St. Louis, Missouri. I was surprised to be accepted by Principia, but uncertain how we could afford it.

With her usual determination, Mother decided that, if I was accepted, it must be for a good reason, and we'd find a way to make it happen. (It was her example of faith in God for guidance that I later followed.) The plan she came up with was that the three of us, including Jewell, would move to the college town of Elsah, Illinois, and Mother would find work there to support us. Besides my attending the college, she hoped Jewell might somehow be able to attend the Principia Upper School for her last two years of high school (which she did).

We paid for my first quarter, and Mother applied for a job at the college. But there were several problems. A job had not yet been confirmed, and we didn't have enough money left to pay for the train fare. I recall that there was a lot of quiet prayer in our household about that situation.

The day before we had to make final decisions about what to do, a woman who'd mentored me as a Republican Party precinct worker came into the bakery with another woman. She introduced her friend as Iolani Ingalls, a professor she knew at Principia.

"Joanne," Miss Ingalls said, "I hear you're attending Principia this fall. It's a long drive for me. I was wondering if you three could accompany me in my car." It was like a miracle: a perfect answer to our prayers! A door had opened to a very different life experience.

At Principia, I became active in the International Relations Club, which led to participation in Model United Nations programs. Eventually, I was appointed the Midwest Regional Director for the Collegiate Council for the U.N., and grants from the Principia School of Nations supported my attendance at C.C.U.N. leadership conferences. After graduation, while attending a conference in New York City, I called my mother, who was still working at the college.

"Mom, I want to stay in New York. I know the school expected me to work in the summer session, but if I go back, I don't know when I'd again have enough money to come back to New York."

"But you don't have enough money to live in New York," my mother reasoned with me.

"I have $50 left, and Ginny (the administrator for the conference) said I could stay in her apartment until I get a job. You know I've always wanted to live in New York City." After further discussion, my mother gave up trying to convince me, and I stayed.

I quickly found a part-time job and then later worked for the American Association for the U.N., helping to organize model U.N.s on college campuses across the United States. It was exciting to work alongside Eleanor Roosevelt and various ambassadors, while attending receptions in Washington, D.C. and at the United Nations.

Eventually, I felt I wanted to do something more meaningful, and my college major of sociology geared me into a new direction. By then, I was living at the 51st St. YWCA. As President of the residence hall, I attended a YWCA Conference, where I was recruited to become a Program Director at the Brooklyn YWCA, later getting a Master's degree in Social Work.

It was at the YWCA that I met Walter, who was part of a Belarusian Youth group meeting there. He was finishing his college years at City College of New York (CCNY), after a stint in the

Army, overseas. Our marriage started a new adventure, leading me to reach another of my dreams: living in Europe in the 1960s. And now we were living back in Europe again.

A realization came: I'd already shifted my self-image along the way, from farm girl to college student, to New Yorker, to suburban mother and businesswoman, and recently, to international traveler. Rather than feeling limited by past background or experiences or self-image, I prayed to be open to fresh ideas, teeming with new possibilities.

Family Reunion at the Monroe farm

16
PACIFIC NORTHWEST FAMILY ROOTS REVISITED

I was excited as Walter turned off Highway 203, onto Ben Howard Road. Our family farm was already in sight. The driveway threw up dust as we approached the farmhouse, and several dogs barked at our arrival. Hearing the ruckus, blond, ever-smiling, petite Bettie (my sister-in-law) came out to greet us, her apron flying in her rush.

"Jo, it's great to see you guys!" I'd almost forgotten that my family often referred to me as "Jo." Bettie grabbed me in a hug.

"Walter, how are you?" She was a little more cautious with him, patting his arm. My relatives really like Walter, but I think sometimes they're not quite sure how to accommodate his more formal European demeanor.

Bettie's sturdy son, good-natured Russ, and his wife, Rhonda, came ambling over from their house across the field. Bettie's younger son, Jeff, planned to arrive later, after picking up her daughter, Claudia, who'd flown in for the family reunion from her home in California.

"How ya doin', Uncle Walt?" Russ said, with a strong handshake. After a hug for me, he started quizzing Walter on what was happening in Belarus. Russ seemed genuinely interested in tapping this contact with someone living in the midst of changing world events. It helped Walter relax, too, in the somewhat unfamiliar environment of farm life.

The next day, the family gathering began. Cars started to arrive, with more dust and barking and hugging. It was so good to see my slightly younger sister, Jewell: she had short, grey hair now, rather than her childhood signature long braids. The majority of the nearly 50 people arriving were related to Jewell's five children: Dan, Kathy, Mark, Tammy, and John – all of whom had children, some even grandchildren.

Jewell was at the reunion with her third husband, Harold. Her first husband and father of her children was Gene, who died after a long illness. She had been the main family breadwinner for many years, often working as a pastry chef. Hers wasn't an easy life; I've admired the fact that Jewell kept a sunny and positive disposition, stemming from a strong spiritual base, even through her challenges.

Seeing Jewell made me think about our childhood. We grew up with our older sister Pat's children, Harold and Sandy, who were almost our own age. They visited the farm often from Seattle, where they lived. I remember being a little jealous that, in the city, they could roller skate and bicycle on sidewalks.

Pat and Bill were officially our half-brother and half-sister, but we always just thought of them as our big brother and sister. Mother's first husband died when the children were young. As a widow, she earned a living by starting a secretarial service from her home on Phinney Ridge in Seattle.

Later, she met and married my then-prosperous older father. (He was almost 60 years old when I was born; Mother was in her mid-forties.) Mother was probably hoping to have an easier life. Unfortunately, the Great Depression changed circumstances when my father lost his Seattle apartment buildings and savings.

My dad had been a genuine pioneer. At 16, he rode in a covered wagon with his family into Indian Territory, in the last big Homestead Run of 1893. The family established a homestead outside of Ralston, Oklahoma and farmed it. He sold that property during the start of the Dust Bowl years in the Great Plains and moved to Seattle. Farming was what my father knew best; so, with money from the sale of some of Mother's Seattle properties, they purchased the farm near Monroe. Actually, it was probably a wise move because, as hordes of unemployed people swamped downtown Seattle looking for work, we were at least eking out a living on a self-sufficient farm.

For Mother, it must have been a traumatic change. She had to leave her beloved Seattle city life for an arduous farm existence. I'm not sure she ever totally adjusted.

As more people arrived at the farmhouse, the noise level – with babies screaming, toddlers joyously shouting, and adults trying to talk over the clamor – became louder than Walter and I were used to. Walter squirreled himself in the living room with a book for awhile, since he was not comfortable with what he called "small talk." Meanwhile, I reminisced about childhood memories around the kitchen table with those that shared my experiences.

Jewell philosophized, "You know, we both got what we wanted out of life. I remember, even in high school, you always talked about wanting to travel to Europe. And now you're actually living there. I just wanted to have a large family around me."

"You sure have that. I feel strange, compared to your crowd, with only two unmarried sons."

Jewell and I are very different. She exudes a quiet, nature-loving disposition, and I am an outgoing organizer and people person. When young, since I was a year and a half older and often told to "look after your sister" out in the yard, I probably bossed her around a bit. I know she remembers getting spanked for activities that she blamed me for starting. That relationship has shifted to mutual respect, in adulthood. I love that she continues Mother's tradition of handwork, making quilts and afghans. Everyone in the family has at least one of her treasures. Jewell is now a Christian Science Practitioner, bringing healing prayer to those in need.

After the potluck picnic, most of the younger crowd with small children left. The rest of us sat around the fire pit, moving around, as the smoke changed direction with the wind. This was the quieter time. Walter was brought into the conversation more, as those interested in our lives probed to get a feel for experiences so far removed from theirs. I took out my notes and a photo album and shared some of the details of our trip behind the Iron Curtain. Someone said, "Wow, you ought to write that up."

A few days after the family gathering, we headed to the airport for our flight back to New Jersey, and then to Munich. In the air, I had time to again think about my farm childhood, the path my life had taken, and the need to make a final decision about a new direction for my life in Europe.

I acknowledged that my farm experience had engendered in me qualities of independence, self-reliance, and a good work ethic. As small children, Jewell and I were expected to help with the farm work: weeding the vegetable garden, bringing in wood for the stove, feeding the chickens, and helping with the canning.

But I could now easily recognize the seeds of my shifting to a different lifestyle. Even when I lived on the farm, I wasn't totally comfortable there. I never did like the bugs and dirt and stinky outhouse associated with farm life; I preferred things to be neat and clean and orderly.

In identifying closely with my city-oriented mother, and appreciating the exposure she gave us to more cultural activities, I had, indeed, even as a child, begun to veer toward wanting exotic, non-farm experiences. I could see that the pivotal point had been my audacity in applying to an expensive college, far from the farm. It was there that opportunities opened, which would not have been available if I'd attended a college in my old environment.

But I also recognized that persistence in pursuing the daydreams of childhood had played a role in realizing them. That was part of what my pioneering father had instilled in me: he called it "gumption."

As we started to descend for a landing in Munich, I closed my eyes to shut out the distractions of landing instructions and thought about the future. I felt a calm assurance about shifting my focus now toward building a business in Italy.

Part Two

OUR WORLD
REARRANGES ITSELF

Florence, viewed from Piazzale Michelangelo

17
SHIFTING FOCUS TO TUSCANY

Upon our return from the States, I organized a plan to build up our marketing business in Italy.

We had started our American business back in the 1970s, naming it Interdiam. Our supply company, Amway Corporation, was an early promoter of environmentally-sound products. At that time, I was on the Environmental Commission in Mountain Lakes, where many homes had septic tanks, and run-off into the town's lakes created a problem of algae bloom. Thus, I was eager to promote Amway's biodegradable detergents, which would help alleviate the problem. (Later, Amway became an e-commerce business. It then distributed not only its own manufactured lines, like Artistry cosmetics and Nutrilite food supplements, but also products from other companies, ranging from furniture to business gifts, and services such as MCI and real estate referrals.)

These products and services were distributed through networks of individual distribution points, rather than the then-traditional route of selling through stores. Thus, an independent business, marketing Amway's lines, could be started without a large capital outlay, as a part-time activity.

Walter and I built our Interdiam business as a team, each of us taking on different roles. Walter did business presentations, planned larger seminars, and developed strategy. I handled product areas and small training activities. Because of my experience as a social group worker, I especially enjoyed enabling others to expand and enhance their options in life. Therefore, I relished organizing courses in goal setting and self-image development.

In the United States, Walter and I achieved a recognized level of success, called Direct Distributors, and, simultaneously, we helped others develop independent businesses too. It was the additional income from this part-time business that allowed us to live in a community with an excellent school system – and therefore high taxes.

When the supply company opened a warehouse in Italy, we decided to expand our own business there. Soon after, in the fall of 1987, I traveled to Italy with other associates and started a number of Italian contacts in our business. A year later, however, our business hadn't grown much beyond initial enthusiasm because there wasn't yet a strong support system in the newly opened market. So, in October of 1988, soon after we first arrived in Munich, Walter and I rented a car and took a long-weekend trip down to Italy to determine if our business there was viable. On the trip back, I asked,

"What do you think about the Italian market, Walter?"

"It looks like a good start; it makes sense to develop it," he answered, encouraging me to think that we'd be working together there.

Several days later, however, Walter threw me a curve ball that I wasn't sure I could handle.

He looked up from reading his daily reports, and said,

"Joanne, I've been thinking . . . that quick three-day trip to Italy was exhausting for me. It took a lot of energy and has affected my concentration at work since then. I don't think I can continue doing that."

"What do you mean?" My voice was rising in alarm. "I thought we agreed the business was worth developing. What are you saying, that I would have to do it alone?"

"Yes, I'm afraid so. I can't keep going down, and I can't divert my attention from work, even to think about it. If you want to do it, go ahead; just don't distract me with the details." And he went back to reading his reports.

"Oh, wow," I said, sitting back, feeling like I'd been slapped in the face.

Okay, I thought, so what do I do now? He's just put the whole responsibility for building a business in a foreign country on my shoulders. I inwardly groaned with the weight of the idea, and my face furrowed near tears. Since our last trip there, I'd had my heart set on being able to enjoy more of the vitality of Italy.

Over the next few days, I felt a lot of personal turmoil, as I decided two things. One, I didn't really know if I could build a successful business by myself, and two, I loved being in Italy enough to try.

I struggled through that first year, taking the eight-hour train trip back and forth to Italy, staying in different hotels in Florence and Rome, and interviewing people who answered my newspaper ad: "Looking for English-speaking persons capable of developing an American business in Italy."

Many obstacles were quickly encountered. For one thing, I was an American woman who did not speak Italian. Cultural differences also entered in: Italian men often ended interviews with, "Would you like to have dinner with me?" totally disregarding that a woman might be a serious business representative. Another response was, "Italians wouldn't be interested in this kind of business, with home delivery; we prefer to shop at our friendly local stores." Also, although I had a registered Italian business, I did not have an Italian business address, so potential associates wondered about my availability to help them get started.

Early results came in Florence, where I was finding people of varying interests, ready to join our business.

Inga, for example, was a progressive German. She said, "I lived in the United States back in the late '60s. I really like American ideas. I'd like to give it a try."

Edoardo was an Italian businessman who had introduced the use of Visa credit cards to Italian banks, and so he was open to new ideas. When interviewed, he said, "I'd be interested in the larger concept of expanding networks of business associates throughout Italy."

Margot, a Swiss, said, "I think my massage clients and gymnastic classes would appreciate the nutrition products. As a single mother, I could use the extra income to finance my son's schooling."

Valeria was a sophisticated Florentine matron, who'd lived for several years in England. She stated her interest, "Florence is such a fashion-conscious city. I think the image consulting part of the business should do well here."

Dianne was an American, married to a Florentine lawyer. "I enjoyed the image consulting part of the business that you presented at the American League meeting, Joanne. But my main interest would be in developing business networks." Dianne was now a mother of two, but formerly she had been an opera singer, model, and modeling agency owner. She seemed to understand, better than most of the others I interviewed, the concepts of goal setting and self-image development. I was encouraged to have a synergistic American on my team.

After a few months, I felt that I'd made a good start at building a business base in Italy, and I enjoyed my widening variety of contacts there. I also loved the wonderful energy of the Italians. The shop owners often sang arias as they worked and greeted me with a smiling, "Buon giorno." Yes, it was chaotic on the roads, and I'd been pickpocketed several times. But the loving, two-kiss greetings, with hugs from my new friends, and our three-hour noisy pizza gatherings warmed my heart.

I often felt lonely, though, being separated from my husband so much. But my need to prove I could accomplish something worthwhile on my own, coupled with my desire to be in Tuscany, kept driving me to return.

Then two things changed, allowing me the opportunity to establish a stronger base for the Italian business.

One evening in Munich, I approached Walter with an idea:

"Hon, since the house in Mountain Lakes is finally sold, what do you think about using some of that money to invest in our business in Italy? Renting an apartment would make building the business there much easier for me."

"That makes sense," Walter replied. "I've also been thinking about buying a car, maybe even a motor home. That rented motor home we used for the Eastern European trip was so convenient."

"Great idea," I replied. We agreed that, with six weeks of vacation time, a motor home would also be a practical mode for vacationing around Europe.

I was thinking, Wow, I hit the jackpot here. Though, now, I'm really going to have to produce better financial results to justify all this expense.

Sharing ideas with business associates

18
CAN I BUILD A SUCCESSFUL BUSINESS IN ITALY?

The decision to buy the motor home and lease an apartment in Florence was a substantially larger commitment, on our part, to the business in Italy. It gave me a viable Italian business address and also the flexibility to expand beyond the cities of Florence and Rome.

Although these investments should increase our chances, I still knew that success wasn't guaranteed. In fact, the greater commitment placed much more pressure on me to produce results, and I wasn't sure of my ability to do so. After all, our success in the States had been a joint accomplishment, with Walter handling major parts of the work.

Two weeks after purchasing a German Dethleff motor home – and after a hug and a "Be careful now" from Walter – I started on the eight-hour trek to our newly rented apartment on Via de

Sanctis in Florence. I was travelling on Sunday to avoid the usual heavy truck traffic over the main southern route through Innsbruck to Italy. It was not only a time of changing scenery, but also of self-questioning and shifting my focus.

The scenery went from cows munching quietly on lush green Bavarian farm pastures, to steep hillside castle ruins near Austria's Innsbruck; then, I was tensing over the dizzying height of the Europa Bridge; before finally coming down into the Italian Alto Adige region, with its vineyards, apple orchards, and colorful, red-roofed Italian villas.

As I ordered pasta and a fresh-squeezed orange juice at the highway rest stop, the chatter of soft-rolling Italian made me smile. The guttural German had been left behind. I knew I was headed into a very different environment.

Coming into the flat Po valley, I no longer needed to be as vigilant in driving. My thoughts began to wander to the tasks ahead: getting new business cards made up, putting an ad in the newspaper, and organizing the living room as an interview/office/training area.

Nagging doubts of possible failure crowded in, including that familiar, You're just a farm girl from the Northwest, what makes you think you're capable of building a successful business in Italy? Another suggestion: You've never done many of the tasks that Walter did in the business. In a new market, where can you turn for help?

I quickly stifled these anxieties by thinking that I would just take it one step at a time and trust that I could grow naturally into each new role. Then, I supported that idea with the affirmative prayer: God, guide me with whatever ideas are needed at the right time.

In driving the last long stretch between Bologna and Florence over the Apennine Mountains, where the highway narrows, vigilance was again needed. There were both light-flashing German drivers trying to edge me over and fast-weaving Italian drivers, as well as a few lumbering trucks illegally starting out on Sunday.

Finally, as I started down the other side of the Apennines into Tuscany, a big smile spread across my face. The Tuscan hills around Florence had always felt like my soul-home. I basked in the shapes and colors of that Tuscan scene: the soft blue-gray olive orchards, spiked with sharply rising dark green cypresses, contrasting with the umbrella-shaped pines. The tower of a castle-like villa came into view, with its earth-toned ochre walls and burnt red sienna tile roof. Since I'd been color-analyzed as an "autumn", I recognized that this Tuscan scene was in "my colors": warm, deep, and subtle. I thought, Maybe that's partly why I feel so comfortable in Tuscany.

I spied several sheep, nibbling hillside grasses. And from my open window, I heard a dog barking after children at play. Driving through that last dip of the mountain into Florence, my weariness was replaced by anticipation. Suddenly the city of Florence, in its bowl-shaped valley, lay before me like a round jewel.

Arriving at the apartment, I found a parking spot near the Arno River, and I appreciated the view out toward the *Ponte Vecchio* (old Bridge). After a few treks up and down with my luggage, I flopped onto the bed and slept until late the next morning.

The next day, I explored my new neighborhood. I was glad to find that there was somewhat upscale local shopping on our street. Around the corner was Massimo's Salon. (Massimo, indeed, became my hairdresser, and, for awhile, he added our image consulting program to services his shop provided.)

I knew I wasn't going to have much time to cook, so I was relieved to find a couple of excellent sources of quick, but delicious, food nearby. Across the street was the delicatessen Convivium (later it moved to Viale Europa), which immediately tempted me with oozing gorgonzola dolce and *vitello con tonno* (cold veal with a creamy tuna sauce). Later, I found a rosticceria near Piazza Gavinana, which had sumptuously spiced rotisserie chicken and crispy grilled polenta. Food was definitely an important ingredient of my enjoyment of Italy. I never experienced what Americans might call a "greasy spoon" restaurant there.

The week after I'd arrived at the new apartment, the telephone rang one morning, surprising me, since only a few people knew the number.

"*Pronto* (Hello)." I had learned the proper telephone reply.

"Buon giorno, Joanne. *Valeria qui* (This is Valeria)." Did you remember that the first Tuesday of the month is the American League meeting? Are you planning to come to the Park Palace Hotel this morning?"

"Thanks for reminding me. Sure, I'll see you at ten."

Valeria had sponsored me to become a member of the American League. The members of this prestigious Florentine charity club were mainly American women married to Italian men, as well as some international and Italian women. The luncheon meetings often included speakers on some Italian historical or cultural topic. I enjoyed expanding my knowledge in these areas – and speaking English was a welcome respite for me, as I usually lived in a sea of flowing Italian.

Since I'd been involved in several community groups in the States, this organization provided me with a familiar outlet in a familiar language and gave me good contacts in the community. Eventually, I contributed to the group as their representative to the International Federation of Women's Clubs, and I shared my specialty programs with them in the area of goal setting and image consulting. Being a part of the American League helped to fill the void of loneliness I felt in Florence, without Walter.

My business skills did, indeed, continue to develop with each step, as the needs grew. At first, the work was mainly my own activity of interviewing and training small groups of associates. Because of my special interest, image consulting, with sales of cosmetics, became a large portion of the business. As more associates desired to enlarge their business activity, I developed an outline they, too, could follow in interviewing new associates. The new associate would at first sit beside me, learning, as I interviewed their first few contacts. Then I'd sit quietly as they made their maiden attempts, until they felt comfortable working on their own. My role shifted to include counseling, as local leadership took on more responsibility.

Many Italian associates were unfamiliar with American goal setting and self-development concepts, which we used from inspirational books such as Norman Vincent Peale's *The Power of Positive Thinking* and James Newman's *Release Your Brakes*. It was gratifying to see their gradual awareness grow. I remember one of the sessions where we talked about the role of the sub-conscious in our actions. I looked up and saw tears of recognition in an associate's eyes.

She said, "I just realized that I've been subconsciously sabotaging my progress. I'm going to stop inputting negative garbage into my thinking about all my shortcomings, and instead try to focus on building on my strengths." "Good," I said. "It might help to make a list of all your good qualities, skills, and accomplishments. Then refer to that list when you need to remind yourself."

After the session, another participant shared, "Joanne, I'm so excited about the idea of making positive affirmations to achieve goals in all areas of my life, not just in the business. How's this one? I am patient with ... (her child). I listen carefully to him and praise good behavior."

"Good start," I replied. Then, I encouraged her to come back next week with a present-positive affirmation in each area: personal, social, financial, health, and business, as well as the one she'd shared about her family.

These positive responses to my programs made me feel I was impacting lives beyond just offering a financial opportunity.

However, trying to build an American-style marketing business in a foreign country teemed with challenges.

For one thing, I needed to adjust to different cultural traits in Italy. Punctuality was not one of them, and I often had overlapping interviews. I never did adjust well to the more relaxed Italian view of time. For instance, evening meetings were scheduled late, and often didn't start until nearly 10 p.m., making midnight the usual ending time. Of course, Italians often caught up with sleep during their afternoon siestas.

In the beginning, I did attempt to learn Italian. I took lessons, used a dictionary, and tried to say different Italian phrases. But several of my business colleagues continually laughed at my bad pronunciation. I just didn't hear the differences and therefore couldn't reproduce the words.

One language experience in the Rome train station is remembered with chagrin:

The train arrived late, and I was relieved to see one of those three-sided telephone cubbyholes right next to the track, so that I could call my appointment. Since the station was known for its high rate of thievery, I carefully placed my business bag tightly between my legs as I dialed, and I wrapped the long strap of my purse securely around my hand.

Suddenly, I was aware that my business bag was being pulled away. I slammed the phone down, grabbed my purse, and sped down the passageway after the dark-haired young man with my bag. I was yelling, "Thief, thief" in Italian, wondering, Why doesn't someone respond to help me? Passersby just seemed to be looking at *me* quizzically.

Since that wasn't working, I forcefully shouted in English, "That's *my* bag. You put it down, right now!" The thief set my bag on the ground and just kept nonchalantly walking away. I grabbed my bag and leaned against the wall in relief. Later, when I told my Italian friends about the experience, they couldn't stop laughing. I had mistakenly used the Italian word *lardo* (fatty) rather than *ladro* (thief). They told me I was actually running after the thief, yelling, "Fatty, Fatty."

The final straw with language attempts came when I was asking for cream at a local store. I'd always had trouble between saying "pane" for bread and "panna" for cream. However, this time, the man behind the counter seemed quite taken aback by my request, almost recoiling in shock, stammering for me to repeat what it was I wanted. I pointed to the cream, and he seemed relieved.

When I told a friend about the experience, she asked, "What word did you use?" Evidently my "panna" sounded more like "pene". My friend giggled nervously, and explained that it sounded like I'd innocently asked the gentleman for his private body part.

Since it was clear that my mispronunciations could get me into big trouble, I decided that that was the end of my attempts to speak Italian, except for greetings, such as Buon giorno and Arrivederci.

Other challenges involved extensive traveling. Initially, after buying the motor home, I started enthusiastically spreading the business further afield, eventually supporting newly established business from Venice to Sicily. But that had its drawbacks. I remember one day in Varese, near Lake Como. I'd spent five hours driving there. Just before the appointed time, I drove up to the associate's home – only to find that she'd switched the presentation meeting to a larger house, and gone there earlier. Her son's directions were not very good and, an hour later, I finally arrived. The large gathering was just breaking up, and the hostess was very distressed with me. I was distressed too: I had another five-hour trip to get back to Florence. I decided that maybe I should pull back to just work in the cities and let local associates travel farther afield.

Gradually, the general business atmosphere in Italy improved. Materials were being produced in Italian, and stronger supportive leadership became available. Although I'd felt very alone at times in the beginning, Joe, the son of an affiliated leader from the States, moved to Milan and came once in awhile to support a growing business in the Florence area.

Joe's handsome, dark-haired, smiling face delighted the women in our group, but he was especially welcomed by the Italian men, who still found it easier to relate to a man when discussing business. And, contrary to initial statements, Walter did give me counsel, and sometimes also traveled down to Italy on a long weekend to support special activities.

Joe's parents, Pete and Barbara, came from the States periodically to share their expertise as well. They brought a wider professionalism, since they were building their businesses all around the world. Their weekend seminars included international speakers, who gave invaluable information and increased enthusiasm for the business. Later, they helped establish a business office in the Florence area.

Pete and Barbara became instrumental in developing strong Italian leadership. The key leaders were Massimo and Elisabetta, a dynamic young Italian couple with great vision. They shaped the expertise of Pete and Barbara into a vibrant Italian business, which gave our more foreign-oriented group the example they needed of strong Italian leadership.

This younger grouping often mixed fun with work. I remember one ski seminar in La Thuile, on the French border. Walter and I skied the sunny slopes all day, picking our way down the mountain, depending on whether we wanted the challenge of jumping steep moguls or taking relaxed curves of joy on the treeless slopes. Walter even skied over the top of the mountain, down into France. Later, we were inspired by a late-afternoon seminar; then we shared ideas around the hot tub and had a delicious Italian dinner, before spending the evening discoing with the younger crowd until the wee hours. We were building memories to long cherish.

During several years of working with our business in Italy, the makeup of the leadership gradually shifted. At first, the leaders were mainly foreign women. Then, more Italian women became associates. Later, some of the husbands joined also, as they saw their wives' success. As the business shifted toward e-commerce, entrepreneurial younger men and women joined the activity. At one point, as an Italian Direct Distributor, I gave an inspirational talk to a business group of over a thousand people. Several of those who'd started with us earlier – Dianne, Margot, and Inga – had, by then, also acquired that same status as leaders.

My personal confidence and work skills had gradually increased, while establishing a successful business in Italy. Deep, caring friendships developed with many associates. I'd found a worthwhile and satisfying purpose for my life in Europe.

John and Steve in Prague

19
OUR SONS EXPERIENCE EUROPE

We hoped that John and Steve would use the opportunity of our living in Germany to visit and travel around Europe. I felt that might also give them a better appreciation of their father's heritage. But I learned that although traveling in Europe had been my dream, it wasn't necessarily theirs.

Both boys had traveled to Europe before. Our older son, John, went on a three-week teacher-chaperoned school trip to Europe, when he was 14. And Steve had backpacked around Europe after high school graduation with his friend, Oliver.

In the summer of 1990, while Steve was on break from college, Walter arranged for him to participate in an in-service training program at the Radios. Steve was looking forward to making a good income in a summer job – with a plan to save some for the school year. Unfortunately, after his arrival, we learned that employees' children could not be paid by the Radios. His father did pay him an allowance of $50 a week, but Steve found it inadequate to enjoy an expensive city like Munich. The work wasn't exciting – it was mainly cataloging material – but Steve admitted, "It's a fun place to work, with all the different languages, armed guards, and the excitement of breaking news stories."

Steve stayed with us and bicycled around Munich on his time off, especially enjoying the nearby Englischer Garten. I knew he'd been on his own for several years, so I was really trying to let go of my overprotective mothering habits. Sometimes, when he was going into town for what sounded like drinking at a Gaststatte, I actually held myself back and didn't caution him to not overdo it (a self-restraint not easy for me).

After his internship was finished, Steve joined us on our third trip into Eastern Europe. First, we headed toward the Berlin Wall. We did this soon after the Wall had been breached, but before East Germany was integrated back into one German state.

When we got to Checkpoint Charlie, Steve took a hammer from the motor home and approached the famous Berlin Wall. He joined the many people chipping away for their "piece of the Wall." He blurted out, "This is something, Mom, to be here, right in the middle of history happening!" History had been Steve's major at Rutgers. I admit it was thrilling for me, also, to see people walking freely from East to West in Berlin, after having felt the repressiveness of East Berlin, during a trip there in the 1960s.

"Look, I bought a Soviet army hat," Steve said, as he plopped the cumbersome hat, with its large red star, onto his head. Walter frowned, obviously not comfortable with his Belarusian son wearing a Soviet hat. The Soviet soldiers were still holed up in their barracks in East Germany, where they were left without a mission.

The Soviet government was reluctant to bring back so many thousands of soldiers, with no jobs waiting for them. The soldiers, however, may have been just as happy to stay there, now with the opportunity to visit West Germany, and potentially to make some cash by selling their gear.

After Berlin, we drove through East Germany into Poland and then northeast to the Bialystok area. That part of the trip was just as dreary as we'd remembered it from the year before, when the country was ruled under Communism. In 1990, it should be remembered, Eastern European countries were still in the process of electing new governments and establishing a new set of laws. Economic development had not yet even begun.

We stayed at a hotel in Belavezha, the same town where we'd been bugged the previous year. Steve asked,

"How much was the room?"

"It was $29 for us, but the locals only pay $3." Walter explained that those differences, between what Westerners were charged and what citizens paid, were a holdover from Communist times. Steve was getting a sense of those times. That increased when we stopped at a local store to replenish the motor home. We bought so many of the items in the scantily stocked store, that he felt concerned we hadn't left enough for the local customers.

On the weekend, some Belarusian students organized a large campfire activity at a *Skansen*, a working reproduction of a typical 19th century village. Later, Steve reminisced about that event:

"Hey, Mom, I got a kick out of being able to toss my sleeping bag on the top floor of that ancient windmill and stay overnight with those students. I remember that the squeaking of the rotating mill vanes kept me awake for awhile. It was really neat; everybody singing Belarusian folk songs, while huddled around the evening campfire."

From Belavezha, we drove south, through the rolling Polish farmlands. Then, we crossed the high, snow-capped Tatra Mountains, and drove down toward Prague. We were headed for the relatives' chata in Vyzlovka. This was to be Steve's first meeting with our Czech relatives.

That evening, we sat around the fire pit together, as we'd done on our 1989 trip. Steve joked with the younger relatives: Andulka and Petr, Mira, and his girlfriend, Sarka – by now, they all spoke more English. I sat snuggled up to Walter, happy to see Steve relating so well with his relatives.

After we returned to Prague, those young family members invited Steve to go out pub hopping with them. Even today, they still mention the good times they had with him that evening. In turn, Steve's impression of Czechs, in general, was, "I like them. They seem very friendly toward Americans."

One of the reasons for our stop in Prague was a Conference of Dissidents, which represented countries still under Soviet rule, including Byelorussia (as it was then called). Vaclav Havel, the president of Czechoslovakia, spearheaded the conference. Others attending were Shirley Temple Black, our newly appointed U.S. Ambassador to Czechoslovakia; Robert Novak, the columnist; Paul Weyrich, chairman of the Free Congress Committee; and Garry Kasparov, the Soviet chess Grand Master.

Walter spoke to the gathering about conditions in Byelorussia. Attendees from the other Soviet Republics shared their hopes for the same freedom that the satellite countries had just gained. Behind the scenes, some strategizing took place to help materialize those hopes.

Steve described his observations of the conference: "It seemed an odd cast of characters. The American right-wingers were still talking from a Cold War stance, which didn't seem to jibe with the help the dissidents were seeking."

"And what's with those long-haired, jeans-wearing guys guarding President Havel?" Steve asked. "They certainly don't look like our stiff, blue-suited Secret Service types, but I guess Havel's a pretty casual guy himself."

Walter and I had had several encounters with Havel and found him an interesting contrast to most world leaders. His appearance – with soft blue eyes, thin blond mustache, quiet manner, and often informal attire – was more reminiscent of a frumpy, intellectual professor than the forceful President of a country. His high standing in the world stemmed, not just from his previous strong stand against Communism, but also because of his insistence on rebuilding the moral fiber of the people who were emerging from authoritarian rule.

The pomp of all the flags and important dignitaries at the conference impressed Steve. He said he felt like he was present at an event that might actually change history. "But, Dad," he questioned, "do you think this support will really help the Soviet Republics gain independence?" That was a good question, one that was seemingly unanswerable at that point.

Steve returned to the States from this trip with a greater understanding of what was happening in the changing world of 1990s Europe. It also solidified his appreciation of both his Belarusian heritage and his Czech relatives. (Because of this developed interest, he later helped his father with Belarusian publishing activities, which was very gratifying to Walter.)

John and Steve came back to Europe for two weeks in the summer of 1992. At that time, they were still living together with other Rutgers students, and John had gotten a permanent job as a systems analyst. John's interest in the trip was mainly to travel with his girlfriend, Patti. She had been touring Europe with her sister, who was going home early.

After pert, blonde, hippie-looking Patti arrived in Munich, the three of them took off with backpacks for adventures together. John had taken several years of German in school, and we thought that would serve them well in communicating throughout Europe. First, they went to the rocky beach of Nice, then toured the castles of Austria, saw the glitz of Vienna, and finally went on to Prague.

After a couple of days in Prague, the three of them were headed for the train station with their backpacks to catch the overnight train to Munich. They were walking single file up the narrow side street, with Patti in front, followed by John, and then Steve at the rear.

A car drove by slowly, and several young people yelled out the open window – it sounded like an antiforeigner slur to John. Then, the car came back again. Suddenly, Steve saw what looked like a gun pointed out the window at his brother's head. And then there was an explosion! Looking on in shock, Steve wasn't sure what had just happened to his brother. Thankfully, John was still standing, though now in a cloud of noxious gas.

"Run!" John shouted. And they ran for their lives – to get off that dark empty street, and over to the train station, before anything more happened.

Finally, when they stopped near the train station, Patti asked, "What happened?"

Both John and Steve had inhaled teargas. They were still coughing, as they tried to explain. It was hard to breathe or speak – their lungs were seared, their faces and eyes were burning, and their adrenaline was pumping. They had just survived a frightening attack in Eastern Europe.

All they wanted to do was get out of there. Even when they finally got on the night train, it was hard for them to sleep. John and Steve still felt ill, and all were upset about what had happened.

Walter picked them up at the Munich train station. John was wearing a high purple top hat, one of the normal souvenirs from Prague, in those days. They all looked bedraggled and didn't talk on the way home. Arriving, the three of them exhaustedly tossed their sleeping bags onto the floor. Then, they lounged around the living room in gloom. Patti went to lie down in the bedroom.

"How was it?" I asked. Walter and I expected they'd arrive at our house bubbling with the excitement of a forever-to-be-remembered European trip.

Steve's eyebrows went up in a sort of disgusted look; he grimaced, and said, almost in a whisper,

"It was great . . . until we got tear-gassed."

"What?"

"Yep, I'm never going back to that place," John said with determination. When he makes up his mind, it's set.

"My gosh, what did you do? Did you call the police?"

"No, we didn't want to miss the train by getting involved with the police," replied Steve.

Just as well, I thought. The police remnants from Communist times might use the excuse to hold the Americans. I was so glad they were okay, but realized they must have been really scared, not sure what was happening to them, or what the long-term consequences might be.

"I'm so sorry," I said. "We really hoped you'd have good memories of Prague."

"Well, we don't," said John.

(Neither of the boys went back to Europe again, though Steve still mentions some of his good experiences.)

First Congress of Belarusians of the World, Minsk

20
BELARUS:
WILL INDEPENDENCE BRING FREEDOMS?

During 1990, the rest of the European satellite countries gained their freedom from the Soviet Union. The Baltic Republics of Lithuania, Latvia, and Estonia were the first of the former Soviet Republics to achieve their independence, in early 1991.

Peaceful demonstrations had been the forerunner to declarations of independence in many Eastern European countries. Demonstrations also started in Minsk, the capital of Byelorussia, after discoveries of mass-murder graves in Kurapaty Woods. Another concern of many demonstrators was the lack of quick government response after the Chernobyl nuclear disaster, and the demonstrators demanded truthful explanations and reforms.

The Belarus Service at RFE/RL now had stringers working from inside Byelorussia, so we followed closely what was happening there. Independence came more gradually than had been the case in most of Eastern Europe. In August of 1990, after overtures for independence from the Republics of Ukraine and Georgia, the Byelorussian government declared the Byelorussian Soviet Socialist Republic a sovereign independent state, still allied to the Soviet Union.

Then, in mid-August of 1991, an attempted coup d'etat by hardliners in Moscow nearly reversed the movement toward independence. But Russian President Boris Yeltsin's dramatic stand on top of a tank rallied the people and stopped the coup. During this time, the media in most of the former Republics was still heavily controlled by the government. Quick relay of factual information from RFE/RL studios to populations in the Soviet Republics assisted the calm evolution during and after the coup attempt.

Soon afterwards, on August 25, 1991, the Byelorussian parliament changed the name of the country to the Republic of Belarus, thus formally replacing the previous Russified name. Its status vis-a-vis the Soviet Union was still unclear, however.

In an isolated hunting lodge in the Belavezha forest, in December of 1991, the leaders of Ukraine, Belarus, and Russia met secretly to form a loose alliance called the Commonwealth of Independent States (CIS). Soon, other Republics joined the CIS. Then, on Christmas day, 1991, Mikhail Gorbachev resigned as President of the Soviet Union, the Soviet flag was brought down, and the Soviet Union ceased to exist.

I had a personal reason to be interested in these events. Several of the RFE/RL service personnel had gone back to the newly independent countries to serve in their new governments. For instance, Toomas Ilves, the Director of the Estonian Service, first became the Estonian Ambassador to the United States, and later, the President of Estonia.

When Walter asked me to marry him, he said, "Joanne, if Belarus ever regains its independence, I'd want to go back to help rebuild the country, and I'd expect my wife to go with me."

"Of course," I agreed. In 1960, that seemed easy to say. After all, it was at the height of the Cold War.

With independence for Belarus becoming a reality, I thought, Wow, maybe I'm going to have to make good on my engagement promise. The first question that came to mind was, Am I ready to live in a non-Western society? Having seen the situation in Czechoslovakia and Poland, I wasn't at all sure I could handle living in what, I presumed, was an even more undeveloped Eastern European country. I realized I'd gotten quite comfortable with our life in more prosperous Western Europe.

On the other hand, looking on the positive side of a move to Belarus, I thought, There must be great needs there; surely there would be ways that I could contribute usefully to the country's development. I decided, If it seems like the right idea to Walter, I'm willing to move there.

Later, on a warm spring weekend afternoon in 1993, we were lounging on our Bogenhausen patio, sipping soothingly cool iced tea and reading. I finished my book and looked up to admire the tall soft green bamboo grove that secluded us from neighbors. I heard bees humming busily around my hanging red geranium planters. It seemed like a relaxed time to gently quiz Walter about what was on my mind.

"Hon, you've gone several times now to Belarus, how do you feel the country is developing?" He put his paper down and thought for a moment.

"Well, they've certainly been putting a lot of roadblocks in the way of the Radios office we've been trying to establish. And if the government doesn't allow free media, they won't have free elections, either."

"Okay, but besides the political situation, do you see signs of better living conditions? Is there any free enterprise sprouting up, as we've seen in Prague?"

"I haven't seen any small shops or private restaurants yet," Walter answered. Then he explained that, in contrast to the European satellite countries, it had been several centuries since Belarus had its own representative government for any length of time and that it might take longer for them to develop real freedoms.

"It's hard to tell how things will go, at this point," he added. "We'll have to wait and see." I was relieved that he didn't sound eager to move there yet.

Then, I got the opportunity to assess the situation in Belarus for myself. Walter received an invitation from Backauscyna, a new non-governmental organization (NGO) in Belarus, for us to attend the First Congress of Belarusians of the World. Belarusian leaders would be coming to Minsk from Australia, Argentina, the United States, Canada, United Kingdom, and other countries of Europe. About 1,500 people were expected to attend the week-long event. This would be the first time, since World War II, that many of these people could safely travel to their homeland.

Some invited leaders were hesitant to attend, feeling that the still-Communist-infested government would try to manipulate the event. The country was already independent, though there was a question as to how much true freedom people really had. Attendance at this meeting, we anticipated, might reveal the answer to that question.

Although border crossings into Eastern Europe had become much easier, I'd heard that it could take up to three days just to cross from Poland into Belarus. Walter got around that problem by getting a card from the Belarusian Ambassador in Germany stating that we were traveling in an official car. As backup, he also arranged to give a ride to a historian and his friend from Bialystok who had been given a special entry document into Belarus, allowing them to by-pass the border lines.

We first stopped in Bialystok to pick up our passengers. As we neared the Poland-Belarus border the next day, we indeed saw miles of cars backed up; some people having been there for days. Some had come prepared with tents; others were playing cards at a table they'd brought. Fortunately, Walter checked at the border and found that our special documentation would allow us to drive around the line-up of cars.

Twenty miles later we entered the city of Hrodna. It was encouraging to see the previous Belarusian national symbol of Pahonia (a knight on a horse) painted on what had probably been an old Soviet welcoming sign at the entry to the city. That gave us hope that change was under-way.

Our passengers left us in the next town, Navahradak. It was time for lunch, and we laughed as Walter translated the sign on the only restaurant in town: "Factory production for public feeding." Then we groaned, as we found out that, of the three items listed on the menu, only one was actually available: spicy sausage with cabbage and boiled potatoes – which had been our fare ever since entering Eastern Europe.

Although change seemed sluggish in the provinces, I thought, Surely the country's capital city, Minsk, will be bustling. We arrived in Minsk on a Sunday. Built by the Soviets, Lenin Avenue, the main boulevard, was a six-lane road purposely directed toward Moscow, but we saw only two cars on it. Bustling, it is not, I concluded. Admittedly, during the week, there was more traffic, though many of the cars were black sedans, like the ones we'd seen used as government cars in Prague. Most workers used public transport.

Minsk was almost totally destroyed in World War II and had been rebuilt. Thus the city was new and clean looking. However, most of the architecture was of uninspired concrete, Soviet-style mass construction.

Our Hotel Belarus was on a hill on the other side of town, across the Svislach River. This was where most international visitors stayed. The hotel had a modern exterior, although it was somewhat run-down-looking inside, and not at all up to Western hotel standards. We were glad to see a guarded parking lot to keep our motor home secure.

As we entered the lobby, I saw many journalists and TV crews with cameras. They looked like paparazzi. I wondered who they were expecting – maybe some big Head of State? Suddenly, they came swooping down on us, flashes going off all around. The reporters had heard that the Belarus Director of Radio Free Europe/Radio Liberty would be at this event. I looked back at Walter and saw that he had our dirty laundry bag slung over one shoulder and a plastic food bag in the other hand. With chagrin, I realized that the same image of Walter would appear on TV in the evening, and in newspapers the next day.

Some of the official press reports the next day were not favorable, referring to those attending the Congress as "returning Fascists", the usual term used for those who had fled Communism. Since the media was still quite controlled, those articles raised a question about how warm our welcome really was from the government, even though the event had been government-approved.

As we exited the hotel elevator onto our floor, something struck me as odd. There was a lady sitting at a table, looking official and in charge of things, with papers and a box of keys in front of her.

"Walter, who is she?" I asked, as we got further down the hall.

"She's the Floor Monitoring Lady. There's one on each floor. We're supposed to leave our keys with her when we go out, not down at the desk." (Once, we forgot to give her our key, and she admonished us sternly that we *must* do so.)

"Why?" I asked Walter. "Having someone on each floor doesn't seem very efficient."

"Well, it's the old Soviet way of keeping track of who's in their rooms. In the old days, I suppose it allowed for a search by the authorities when the guests were out. This hotel was mostly used by foreigners, who were always considered suspect."

"Probably they had listening devices in the rooms, too," I said. "I wonder if she'll report our movements to someone." I was always ready for a sense of intrigue.

That afternoon, we headed for the Parliament building: Walter had an appointment with some of the Opposition leaders. When our taxi driver realized that Walter was the Belarusian Service Director, he refused to allow him to pay the fare. "I always listened to you on Radio Svaboda (Liberty)," he said. I was beginning to feel like I'd married a rock star.

This feeling increased in the next few days. Once Walter's face was on TV, and word got out that the Radios' Director was in town, people stopped him along the way, telling him their stories, sometimes about husbands who were in jail, falsely accused, or who had "disappeared." Their hope was that he would air their story on the radio and that it might pressure the government on their behalf, but there were too many such stories to make that hope viable.

The Congress began the next day, held in the Minsk Opera House. This was an imposing building with a rounded entry and much gold decoration. Inside, there were comfortable padded seats in the large hall, and the stage curtain was woven hangings of red and white geometric Belarusian folk designs. The stage arrangement was more austere, with a long table and microphones running down the length of the platform. The scene resembled a formal Soviet Politburo Presidium.

There were several days of meetings, speeches, and many roundtables on history, culture and linguistics. Experts from Belarus shared with experts from the Diaspora. From what Walter translated, it seemed that some of the Diaspora wanted a return to nationalist trappings, whereas locals were more eager to gain economic equality with the West. The Congress adopted many resolutions, most calling for specific democratic changes in the country.

As part of the Diaspora, Walter actively participated in the proceedings, at one point standing to defend some issue about the Radios. He also was a participant on the linguistic panel, a topic that had been important to his father. The Belarusian language had recently been reinstated as the official language of the country, over Russian.

Sometimes there were verbal fireworks in the meetings. One resolution called for the resignation of the Belarusian Defense Minister, who had recently forcefully put down demonstrators in Minsk. The Foreign Minister, Piotr Krauchanka, was seated on the stage. His face became stone-like as the resolution was read. He knew the proceedings were being televised and that this resolution would reflect badly on him. He rose and heatedly threatened the group: "You are guests in our country. People will see this on TV. Something could happen to you for proposing such things." And then he added, "Political harm could come to your countries for your actions." As Walter translated this to me, I thought, It seems we're seeing the government's true colors in this interchange.

There were a number of government-sponsored cultural events planned around the Congress. I especially enjoyed one impressive evening, which included the Belarus Ballet Company and an opera performance – both as professional as one might see in New York City's Lincoln Center. There was also a gala exhibit of Belarusian artists from around the world and a Kupalle summer solstice folk evening.

The government co-sponsors of the Congress organized a banquet at the Hotel Jubilejnaya, toward the end of the Congress. It was meant to be a time for the Diaspora representatives to mingle with government officials, among them the Head of State, Stanislau Shushkevich; the Foreign Minister, Piotr Krauchanka; and the Orthodox Archbishop of the state-run church.

We were enjoying the pomp of the evening, until a local Belarusian alerted us to be careful, because two women at our table were KGB, sent to report on our conversations. (Even though most countries, including Russia, had at least changed the name of the KGB, the Belarusian government had kept the old name – perhaps to continue to place fear in its citizens.) The presence of the two KGB women at our table definitely did *not* leave us with a positive impression of the current government's intentions!

The government had gone to great expense to impress their important Diaspora guests from around the world. One of their main goals was to have the Rada, the Belarusian Government in Exile, officially turn over its mandate to the new independent Belarus government, thus ending opposition from within the Diaspora. However, Rada officials determined that the government still consisted of the same Communists as before, in differently shaded political garb, while not restoring enough freedoms to the Belarusian press and people. Therefore, they felt that their monitoring of the situation remained necessary, at least until more changes were implemented. They refused to recognize the government as legitimately democratic yet.

This was a blow to the purposes of the Belarusian government, as it had sanctioned and supported the Congress. However, we certainly agreed with that decision. And, from what we'd experienced on the trip, I also didn't feel that it was the kind of country in which I'd feel safe or comfortable living, at least not yet.

Are these tomatoes irradiated by Chernobyl?

21
A DARKER UNDERSIDE IS REVEALED

During our stay in Minsk, a number of the activities we attended were not sanctioned by the government, and therefore they revealed much more of the actual situation in Belarus than the officials would have preferred us to see.

One day, several of us went to the headquarters of the opposition party in Belarus, called the Belarusian Popular Front for Renewal. The chairman, Zianon Pazniak, was an archeologist who had gained recognition by discovering thousands of human remains buried in Kurapaty Woods. Pazniak spoke about the injustices still present in the country and urged the Diaspora to continue to pressure Western governments to demand more democratization in Belarus. As various opposition leaders spoke, it was obvious that they were each passionate about their own diverse causes. An important question was, Would they be able to compromise sufficiently to form a cohesive opposition that could win elections?

Later that day, we visited Kurapaty Woods. It was recently acknowledged to have been used as burial grounds for over 100,000 Belarusians, during the 1937-1941 period of Stalinist terror. Pine trees had grown up over what had been an open field. Everywhere there were lumps or indentations in the ground, above the former mass graves. Walking through the woods in quiet memoriam, I felt the weight of those Stalinist years upon me, much as I'd felt the weight of the Holocaust when walking through Treblinka, in Poland.

At the end of the Congress, outside the Opera House, some of the Diaspora group spontaneously set up a large ring, and placed dozens of candles in it, to commemorate the victims of Kurapaty Woods. Having visited the Woods, I was especially moved to feel that those murdered thousands were finally being recognized and honored.

Another visit was to the offices of the Open Society Foundation, an NGO organization, sponsored by the philanthropist George Soros. It was wonderful to see the Director, Liz, who was a friend we had known in Munich. The Foundation was channeling money into Belarus to encourage democracy and free enterprise. They were also helping to update textbooks with more balanced views of the world than had been possible under Soviet rule. Liz was interested in having Walter set up training for Belarusian media personnel about unbiased reporting.

We talked with her about teaching more Westernized ways of thinking to the people in Belarus. We'd trained people with similar programs in our business. Individual thinking and planning had not been supported under the totalitarian control of Communism.

In fact, acting on these basic freedoms might even have been dangerous. Liz was excited about the idea, and Walter and I immediately started talking about how to organize the program.

One morning, Walter greeted me with,

"Joanne, I'm going to be tied up in meetings for a couple of days. I know you'd written to CitiHope about visiting their offices. Why don't you do that, during this time?" CitiHope was an American faith-based organization funneling money and goods to the victims of Chernobyl. Alex, a friend from New Jersey, worked closely with CitiHope, and we'd previously contributed to its cause.

"How would I get there by myself?" I was a bit alarmed at being sent off on my own.

"Give CitiHope a call," Walter answered. "Maybe they can arrange it."

"Okay, I'll check with Delores. She might like to come, too." Delores was an American wife of another Belarusian. It turned out that she was eager to join me because her husband would also be busy elsewhere.

The CitiHope people picked us up in a van the next day. At their offices, they shared with us some background information on the Chernobyl event and explained their work to alleviate the after-effects of the nuclear disaster.

People around the world had heard about the explosion and meltdown at the Chernobyl nuclear plant in Ukraine, on April 26, 1986. I remember the fear generated, even in America, by the news of huge radiation-filled clouds moving around the world. In Mountain Lakes, we bought special soap to wash our vegetables during the early months after the explosion. For years, people in Europe were cautioned not to eat mushrooms or venison because those foods retained radiation for a long time.

Next to the Ukrainian territory immediately surrounding the nuclear plant, the worst-hit country was Belarus because the prevailing winds took the irradiated clouds northwest, over Belarus. The whole nearby area should have been immediately evacuated, of course. Instead, the Soviets denied and hid the event for over a week, until Geiger counters in Scandinavia confirmed that a horrendous radiation leak had occurred.

In the meantime, children in Belarus had been marching all day in the May Day celebrations, with the full strength of the radiation raining down on them. Two million people in Belarus were exposed to tremendously high levels of radiation. Cancers and deformities, especially in children, soared after Chernobyl. Ghost towns arose as 24,000 people were eventually evacuated from the worst affected areas. Some parts of Belarus – around the Homel region – are still officially off-limits to any habitation. Unfortunately, government money has been scarce for resettlement or decontamination of the land, and some of the farmers stayed or moved back.

CitiHope primarily supported the radiation-affected children in Belarus. They flew in planeloads of desperately needed medical equipment, medicine, vitamins, and uncontaminated foods. They also had a program whereby Westerners could sponsor children with monthly payments. CitiHope encouraged people in Western nations to bring children out of the country during the summer months, so that their immune systems could regenerate. For instance, Ivonka, later the President of the Rada, was instrumental in getting the Canadian government to bring children from the Chernobyl area to Canada for the summers.

Since we had been personally supporting the efforts of CitiHope, I was eager to see its operation. A CitiHope official made arrangements with the local government for us to visit some of the orphanages and hospitals where affected children lived. Alla, of CitiHope, accompanied us and translated. What followed was two days of eye-opening trips around the outskirts of Minsk.

Alla stated, "You understand that they will only allow you to visit their *showcase* facilities. Most are much worse." As we progressed on the tour, we noted that even these facilities appeared understaffed, and the nurses we saw seemed overwhelmed with the job of countering the effects of the world's worst nuclear accident.

It was heart-wrenching to walk through the utilitarian, concrete Hospital # 1. As to be expected, there were the usual antiseptic smells of a hospital. In one room, there were dozens of babies in respirators and toddlers hooked up to IVs. In another room, filled with rows of beds, young children looked gaunt, with shaved heads and vacant eyes. Where there were children with terrible deformities, I had to walk past, with my head down; it was just too much for me.

But at the same time, I offered a prayer of gratitude for the doctors and nurses who so selflessly cared for the children's needs. One of the doctors quietly stated his frustration at not having the medicines that could save many of the children. I prayed that the world would find a way to prevent such disasters in the future and also to bring increased help for those affected by this tragedy.

Our next stop was an orphanage. We found one dorm room filled with eight or ten children, all neatly dressed, who were sitting quietly on their beds. Most of the other children had "gone on a field trip," we were told. The severe-looking attendant, saying, "We have good workers," proudly showed us how the forks were neatly stacked in the kitchen. Later, she assured us, "The government has supplied us with everything we need."

I felt inured to being fed propaganda. I would have preferred to have seen more play equipment outside the building, with children running and having fun.

This trip impelled Walter and me to help CitiHope further in their efforts with Belarusian children, both financially and by alerting others who might help. For instance, Don and Harriet, one couple in our business, foster-sponsored a Belarusian child, sending monthly payments and exchanging photos and letters with the family.

At the end of the Congress, Walter and I visited the Minsk farmers' market, the Kamarouka, to stock up on food for the next part of our trip. The market had small tables in rows, with babushka-clad farm women, wearing typical long skirts, selling their various vegetables and accepting money with rough farm hands.

I asked Walter, "How come our line is short and the line at that other table is so long? They seem to be selling the same food. Actually, the tomatoes in our line look even larger." By then, we were already purchasing ours.

"I don't know. Let me ask the fellow over there." Walter came back with a concerned look on his face.

"He said everyone is over there because those vegetables are from the Caucasus, and therefore more surely not contaminated." Then we noted Geiger counters hanging nearby, which were evidently used to check the food from Belarusian farms — since many still produced food with too high a radiation count. I looked at our bag of tomatoes and said, resignedly,

"Oh, well, we don't have to eat irradiated tomatoes every day. Surely, once isn't going to hurt us."

During the time we were in Minsk, we also visited the U. S. Embassy. We got an unvarnished view from a U. S. Information Agency (USIA) representative. He complained of the lack of funds being provided by our government for Belarus. He said most of the Embassy staff (at that time) seemed to feel that knowing Russian was sufficient, rather than having to also learn Belarusian. In fact, he felt it almost seemed, in 1993, that the U. S. still preferred having a monolithic Soviet Union to deal with, rather than the new collection of break-away former Soviet Republics.

Walter's response to this information was to encourage other Embassy staff members of the importance of learning Belarusian, to show respect for the new country. It seemed that our United States government, as well as individuals, was having trouble adjusting to the new realities after the demise of the Soviet Union.

Another Embassy staff member expressed alarm when hearing our plans to spend an overnight in our motor home in northern Belarus, at Lake Narach. He said they usually sent a local driver with anyone needing to travel outside of Minsk. He warned us to at least stay overnight in official campgrounds (we never saw any of those). Car-jacking had become a problem in the countryside, and some car owners had recently been murdered. After leaving the Embassy, I said to Walter,

"Do you think maybe we should change our plans, if it's that dangerous? We could drive directly from Minsk to Vilnia in a day." Vilnia was our next destination on the trip.

"I think they exaggerate the danger. The same kinds of things happen in Prague, but that doesn't stop us from going there."

"Yeah, I guess that's true."

"You know, Joanne, I usually just fly in and out of Minsk. With the motor home, this may be my only chance to see the Belarusian countryside."

"That's probably true. And since you speak the language, it's different than you just being another American traveling through."

So, at the end of the Congress, we left the hotel to travel northwest, through farmland, toward Lake Narach. As we drove by open meadows and swampy areas, I began to relax and digest the events of the last week, contrasting them to what we'd seen happening in Poland and the Czech Republic. Admittedly, in those countries, there was currently much chaos and obvious corruption accompanying the shift from Communism to a democratic society. But, we'd also rejoiced that our friends and relatives no longer had to fear the arbitrary decisions of Soviet authorities. Not only that, but free enterprise was burgeoning, and new laws were being enacted to safeguard people's rights. There was hope, now, in those countries. I certainly wanted the Belarusians to be able to experience these freedoms – but I hadn't seen much evidence of any changes so far.

As we arrived at Lake Narach, I appreciated its very quiet environment. It had been designated a nature preserve. There were no buildings surrounding the lake, just meadows of flowers, edging out to the water. Farther back, there were stands of birch trees, with their stark white tree trunks, accentuated by black flecks and feathery green leaves at the top. Narach is the largest lake in Belarus, so large that strong winds can whip up high, ocean-like waves, endangering fishing boats. But on the day we were there, it was quiet.

We stayed overnight in the motor home by the lake, and we appreciated the break from the intensity of Minsk. It also gave me an opportunity to raise the question upper-most in my mind. I thought I knew the answer, but I needed Walter to articulate it.

"Walter, it strikes me as quite repressive here still, what with the hotel floor ladies monitoring guests, and the KGB trying to eavesdrop on us at the banquet table. Then, there was that threatening outburst of the Foreign Minister at the meeting. How do you feel things are going in the country?"

"Not good. The Communists are still in power. It's a country teetering between gradually gaining more freedoms and slipping back under Russian influence. It's hard to tell what will happen with the next elections." The elections were expected to take place in 1994.

"So, at least for now, you're not thinking about moving here?" I figured I might as well get my worst fears out in the open.

"No. There'd have to be an awful lot of advances for me to live here." He paused a moment and then added, "Anyway, the present government doesn't seem to want Western émigrés returning to Belarus."

"Oh, why do you say that?"

"For one thing, remember my TV interview, earlier in the week? I made some pertinent statements about how returning émigrés could help the country by bringing back their experience with democracy and free enterprise, just as has happened in the Baltic countries. They purposely cut that segment of my interview out of the TV broadcast. And, in many other ways, the government has made it clear they don't want us meddling in their chosen way forward – if it really is forward."

"Really? But that means they'll be missing a key element that has helped other countries jump-start their turn toward democracy."

"Unfortunately, it looks like it, at least for the time being."

Although it didn't seem viable for Walter to move to Belarus to participate in the country's renewal at that time, I knew he'd try to find other ways to facilitate progress for Belarusians.

As much as I was sorry for what all this implied for the Belarusian people, I heaved a personal sigh of relief that we would not soon be moving to a country still so problematically repressive.

Shrine in the ancient gate to the city

22
VILNIA AND ITS DIVERSE HISTORY

Leaving Lake Narach in Belarus, we drove toward Lithuania, with the desire of visiting Vilnia, shown on our map as Vilnius. That was the city where Walter was born and lived for his first eight years, from 1932 to 1941. I'd never heard him speak much about those years, and yet they say that the first five years are the most crucial in a child's development. I hoped that being there would jog some of his memories, so that I could flesh out more of what had shaped him.

As we drove toward Lithuania, I noticed some differences in this more northwestern part of Belarus. The houses in towns were still small wooden frame buildings, but they were more gaily painted than the ones we'd seen in the central area. These houses were yellow, blue, green, or turquoise, and some even had two contrasting colors. More care and upkeep was apparent. I wondered if it was indicative of a more open, Western influence here, as compared to the longer Soviet influence we'd seen farther east in Belarus.

Belarus, Poland, and Lithuania had had very fluid borders over the centuries, with towns sometimes located in one country, then in another. For instance, Walter's first passport stated that he was born in Wilno, Poland, though the language of the majority of the surrounding population, at that time, was Belarusian. Later, with a shift in borders, Vilnia became Vilnius, the capital of Lithuania. The multi-cultural city population – of almost equal parts Jews, Poles, and Belarusians – then shifted, with Lithuanians becoming the majority, as they came for education and government positions.

These thoughts reminded me of an even further removed time:

"Walter, you've always talked so proudly about 'the heyday of Belarusian history,' with the Grand Duchy of Litva (during the 1400s to 1600s when Vilnia was a center of Belarusian culture). What made that era so important?"

"Well, it was a time of great intellectual enlightenment during the Renaissance, and the Grand Duchy was the major Eastern European country in the forefront of that movement."

I'd seen ancient maps showing the Grand Duchy as a combination of lands, including all of Belarus and Lithuania and parts of Poland, Ukraine, and Latvia. Old Belarusian had evidently been the official language.

Walter explained that it was a country whose territory came together through consensus, not war, and its laws were advanced, for that time, including lower nobility in decision making. Culturally, Vilnia was considered a major center of learning in Eastern Europe, with a university established in the 1500s. The Grand Duchy was also one of the first countries where the Bible was translated into the local language, which was a sign of democratization.

The border crossing into Lithuania was not too traumatic. Then, as we drove through the outskirts of Vilnia, I asked Walter,

"I heard someone refer to Vilnia as being the 'Florence of the East.' What did they mean?" Walter explained that Vilnia hadn't been bombed as badly as Warsaw or Minsk and therefore had retained its ancient character, with some similarities to Renaissance Florence in its architecture.

He said, "Before the war, Vilnia was also known as 'the Jerusalem of the East,' because of its large Jewish population." He explained that the city had traditionally been religiously diverse and had Jewish temples; mosques, where descendants of the Tatars worshipped; and Eastern Orthodox, Catholic, and Protestant churches.

After Walter's descriptions, I was really looking forward to seeing this ancient city, with its diverse cultural heritage.

And it did charm me with its Old-World character. We drove into Vilnia on the bridge over the Vialla River (*Wilija* in Polish and *Neris* in Lithuanian). Especially in its center, the city had retained its beautiful buildings: some Gothic, Renaissance, and Baroque. The ancient wall, still standing around part of the city, had been for battlements. (Its old city center is now a UNESCO World Heritage site.) We did see, though, looming out in the distance, some of the Soviet influence: the grey, stark, concrete high-rise apartment buildings, highlighting a recent, less artistic era.

We parked and walked along the narrow, winding cobblestone streets and alleys. At the ancient gate to the city, we were delighted to discover the relief of a Pahonia emblem, which had been a historical symbol of the Grand Duchy of Litva, and was now used by both Lithuania and Belarus.

I looked through archways into lovely inner courtyards. Many of those courtyards had red, orange, and yellow flowers cascading from balconies, brightening the living environment. The houses were of stucco or brick, often in shades of ochre. I recognized the Florentine similarity.

In some places, bullet holes were still visible, illustrating past struggles. At the same time, I heard hammering, evidence of reconstruction. We saw many stirrings of private enterprise in the refurbishing of small boutiques and shops. The café where we ate had the same atmosphere as any café in Western Europe. I sensed a vibrancy and optimism in Vilnia that had not been evident in Minsk.

At the café, I decided to plumb Walter's memories of his early childhood.

"Walter, how were things for you and your family, during those years in Vilnia?"

"Well, I was pretty young. We left when I was just eight, so I wasn't too aware of things outside of home and school. What I most remember was the downtown combination stationery/bookstore that Father opened in order to support the family, after his political career was shortened. Father was around more then, until the war started."

As we resumed our walk, through a round, gated entry to the city, Walter said,

"This was the gate I often went through to get to school. It's called *Vostraja Brama* (The Gate of Dawn)." I saw that it was decorated in friezes and gold trim.

Walter pointed to the top of the gate. "See, up there: it was a shrine, so I had to take my hat off, going under it. It got pretty cold in the winters: once it went down to -40 F. On the cold days, I walked on Subach Street, through the Jewish section of town, so that I didn't have to remove my hat. I liked it better, anyway, because it was a lively area, with many shops and people on the streets."

I knew that Vilnia had been occupied by both the Germans and Soviets during the war. I asked Walter how Vilnia had fared during the Stalinist years.

He said that, from 1939-41, the Soviets were only in control about a year. But then they returned, after the Germans were defeated. It was estimated that during those various occupations, 40,000 residents of Vilnia were exterminated, or sent to the gulags.

"That's horrible. But it must have been bad during the German occupation too, wasn't it?"

"I don't really know about that, firsthand. Certainly, it was worse for the Jewish population. But, soon after the German army occupied Vilnia, in 1941, we left for Prague."

I was grateful that Walter's family had not stayed in Vilnia to experience the Stalinist years of exterminations and transfers to Siberia – although some of the Stankievich relatives had been sent off to gulags.

Brothers Walter, George, and Bill, at Vilnia home

23
FAMILY FLIGHT FROM THE SOVIETS

That first day in Vilnia, we stayed overnight with Belarusian friends. Then, the next day, we drove up a hill on the outskirts of town. One of our reasons for coming to Vilnia was to visit the house Walter remembered living in, as a child. Actually, they'd lived in several different rented houses, but it was this last one, where his memories were strongest.

It wasn't easy to find the house he remembered on Marcova Street. The area was very overgrown, since his time, more than 50 years before. Also, the house had had a fire and lost its second story, so it looked quite different now: with narrow windows, vertical siding, and a tin roof. The haphazard picket fence around the yard was missing several posts. We walked on a well-trodden foot path to the front of the house.

Walter knocked on the door. He explained to the woman who answered that he'd lived there before and asked if we could look around. I think he was hoping she'd invite us inside, but she evidently wasn't comfortable offering that.

As we walked to the back of the house, we looked out on the city and river valley below. Most of what we saw was red tile roofs and many church steeples, among winding streets. Walter stopped and pointed to the valley beyond the city. He said,

"That's where we saw the Soviet troop columns advancing on the city of Vilnia, in mid-September of 1939. It was part of a temporary agreement between Stalin and Hitler. I remember it well, because it was just three days after my birthday."

He said that earlier, in the first days of September, they'd had bombing raids by the Germans, as they invaded Poland. (Vilnia was part of Poland then.) That first time they heard the sirens, Walter was alone in the house with his baby brother, Bill. He ran out with Bill in his arms and pushed him into the air raid trench. They heard the explosion of bombs falling, mostly on the city airfield.

"Bill was crying, and I was pretty scared, myself, though we were comforted by some neighbors. The trench was right down there." He pointed to some bramble bushes, farther down the hill.

"How did you know what to do, being alone in the house?"

"We'd had warning. I remember the old crystal radio we had. We needed to scratch the crystal until we got the right frequency, and then listen up close, to hear the broadcasts. I recall how alarmed my parents were, when it was announced that Germany had attacked Poland. It was soon after that, that the trench was dug, and George and I were told to hide there, if we heard sirens."

"How could your mother leave you alone at that age – what were you, seven or so?"

"Yes. Well, Mother had gone out to check on Father and my

brother, George." His mother had been told by a nearby merchant that the police had taken her husband away, so she immediately went to the jail to try to get him released. The Polish authorities had picked him up in a sweep of Belarusian activists, at the war's outbreak.

Unfortunately, George had been reading in the back of their store, and in the confusion of being arrested, his father had forgotten and mistakenly locked him in. It was several hours later that eleven-year-old George was remembered and let out of the store.

"What happened with your father?" I was wondering if he was in jail long.

"The political detainees were released a day before the entry of the Soviets into the city. That's when Father left quickly. He knew that Belarusian activists would be either sent to the gulags or exterminated." It was too dangerous to take children, so the family was left in Vilnia. Walter paused a moment, as he thought about the life of his mother and brothers under the Soviets in 1939. Then he added,

"Within a week of Soviet arrival in Vilnia, food became scarce, with long lines everywhere. Mother had stockpiled some food. I remember mixing honey with a tub of butter to preserve the butter longer, in the absence of refrigeration."

"I can't imagine going through such times," I said. "It must have been especially difficult for your mother, when your father left."

"I guess it was. One of the problems was that the store had been closed, and Mother didn't have much income. She was glad when we could finally leave for the protection of her family in Prague." By then, Vilnia, as well as Prague, was under German occupation, but at least Prague wasn't in the fighting zone.

From the story Walter told, that trip to Prague wasn't easy. They were sheltered and fed in resettlement camps along the way; many people were being resettled in different directions. He recalled that one camp was a monastery, another was a barracks. Sometimes they traveled in trucks, other times on freight trains.

"Everything was pretty chaotic: it's kind of jumbled in my mind. I know it took us about three months to reach Prague, just a day's train ride away."

The recounting of those travails reminded me of something I'd wondered about.

"Your father's work for Belarusian independence certainly impacted the family strongly. How did he start down that path?" After all, his father had been just a farm boy.

Walter said that, as a teenager, his father was a newspaper deliverer, and then a reporter, for the influential Belarusian newspaper, *Nasha Niva* (our field). Writing about the problems of his countrymen encouraged his desire to help Belarusians gain more freedoms, and he became active in Belarusian organizations.

"And that's what got him into trouble along the way, then?"

Walter acknowledged that. He said that his father had studied for the priesthood, but the Polish Seminary authorities soon asked him to leave because of his Belarusian activism. Scholarships also dried up for Belarusians. That's why his father ended up going to Czechoslovakia on scholarship, in 1922, where he received a Doctorate in Philology at Charles University, and where he also met his wife.

Evidently, he had a good teaching job when he first came back to Vilnia and before starting the family. Then, he was briefly in the Parliament, representing a heavily Belarusian district, until the political situation changed, and the Parliament was dissolved. That was when he opened the store.

"But," Walter said, "whatever the circumstances, Father continued to fight for the right of Belarusians to have their own government."

This side trip to Vilnia had been enlightening in many ways. I appreciated the beauty and the enlivened, progressive atmosphere of Vilnia, in contrast to the still oppressive climate that we'd experienced in Minsk. And I realized that Belarusians who had lived under freer conditions in and around Vilnia – as I had earlier thought – had assuredly had a very different experience and attitude about life than those living farther east, under longer and heavier Soviet control.

During the drive home, I was thinking about the ramifications of some of the things we'd experienced and shared. I was grateful to have seen Walter's Vilnia home and early environs and to hear him share more of his childhood memories. I'd begun to understand better what had shaped Walter. For instance, I'd never sensed too much emotional closeness between Walter and his father. Obviously, his father hadn't been around much in their early lives. Walter, though, certainly had identified with his father's Belarusian patriotism.

I could see that, even with the constant uprooting, Walter's family had strong bonds. I felt that his mother needed to be given much of the credit for that. She was a plucky woman: small of stature, but tenacious. She'd held the family together, often taking courageous steps to secure their safety. During her college years at Vassar, where she was a Czech exchange student, she had become a devout Methodist, and the children were raised with a firm moral base. I could see this reflected in Walter's strong sense of integrity – of right and wrong. During Walter's middle school years, the uncles and aunts in the extended Prague family also provided stability.

Later, I questioned Walter about something that had always

puzzled me. He's intelligent and savvy. But he's very self-effacing. He humbly avoids taking credit, even when he's done a good job. This often bothered me, because it sometimes resulted in others not giving him credit. One day, I asked him,

"Why is it that you are so self-effacing? What's the basis for that quality? Humility is good. But I feel you take it too far, and dismiss deserved praise."

He cogitated that for awhile. Then he told me that it probably went back to the circumstances of his early childhood. He explained that he changed schools often, as a youngster, and was thrown in with different curricula and languages spoken. Although the languages were mainly Slavic and he could quickly learn them, he did not always understand their nuances, so he sometimes didn't do well in tests. Since what he did achieve often wasn't as good as he felt he could have done, praise felt uncomfortable.

But he doesn't let that hinder him. For instance, he will speak up in meetings to say what he feels is the truth of a situation, even when it might be wiser to "let it ride." Some of that quality was evidently fostered during those independent years away from family: at school and at Boy Scout camps in the Displaced Persons camps in Germany.

Understandably, Walter doesn't carry the same attachment to a place, as I do with the family farm in Monroe. Community, to him, means the Belarusian community, wherever it may be, and that bond gives him a strong sense of identity.

Travel was simplified with a motor home.

24
MOVING TO EASTERN EUROPE

The next year, 1994, was an unsettling time at the Radios. Rumors darted at us from every direction. The gist of them was "The Cold War is over. Congress probably won't fund Radio Free Europe/ Radio Liberty anymore."

Walter and I realized we might be leaving Europe soon. He wasn't 65 yet, when he would start receiving full Social Security payments, so we weren't sure what lay ahead.

Gradually, events began to unfold in a new direction for the Radios and in our lives. Although the East European operations of the Radios were being reduced, there was still a need in the former Soviet Republics for continued access to unbiased information.

"Since Munich is an expensive city, maybe the Radios will move the rest of their operations to an Eastern European city like Prague or Riga" was the next rumor.

Czech President Vaclav Havel, a vocal fan of the Radios, convinced the Czech Parliament to lease the former Czechoslovak Federal Assembly building to the United States for a minimal fee. The Radios were then expected to renovate and maintain the building. The building had been vacant since the Czech and Slovak Republics became separate countries.

Because of Walter's facility with speaking both Czech and English, and his understanding of the Radios' needs, he was asked to spearhead the transition of the remaining Radios Services from Munich to Prague. For the next several months, he spent about a week each month in Prague, working with the Czechs to remodel the building and laying out the configuration for the different Services within the new facility. Walter was later honored with a plaque: "For outstanding support in executing the RFE/RL move to Prague."

"Oh, Walter, I'm so glad the Radios are moving to Prague, and not Riga," was my enthusiastic response to the planned move. "Maybe now you can at least help with translating for the business in Prague; I'm not finding that market very easy." I'd already started laying the groundwork for a business there.

"Well, I was thinking, there are a couple of things we need to do to make this transition and the work easier," Walter said. One was getting another vehicle. We chose a Ford Escort, hoping it wouldn't attract as much attention as a BMW. At the time, almost half of the foreign cars being driven into the Czech Republic ended up being stolen. We weren't as worried about the motor home because it was more easily identifiable.

The other suggestion was to rent an apartment in Prague, which would then be our third home in Europe: in Munich, Florence, and now Prague – making for interesting business cards, since we also still had a business address in the United States.

The motor home became even more important to me, as I traveled between our different locations. For instance, the drive from Prague to Florence required two days, so I was grateful to be able to choose a lovely Alpine setting for the overnight stay inside the motor home. Walter used the new car for his five hour drive from Munich to Prague.

Since most housing had not yet been released for personal ownership, we were grateful that a friend of our relatives had a furnished panelak apartment on Marikova, available for us to rent. As we walked through it, we realized that the inside of the prefabricated concrete apartment house was even worse than the ugly exterior.

"Yuk, Walter, what is that smell?" I asked, as I put my hand over my nose. The odors of spicy sausage and acrid cabbage overwhelmed me. Walter found the reason: the bathroom had a large hole in the ceiling and floor, through which the pipes for bath and kitchen ran – and which also circulated the odors of the entire apartment house.

During that first year of living part-time in the Marikova apartment, life was quite dreary. The Czech Republic was not recovering very fast from the Communist era. Only small areas of privatization showed vigor, and not much reconstruction was apparent yet. For me, bright moments included Walter coming to Prague and several visits from American business associates Don and Harriet, who were also building a business in Eastern Europe. Don was of Czech background and delighted to have a reason for frequent visits.

In September of 1995, Radio Free Europe/Radio Liberty moved its remaining broadcasting operations from Munich to Prague.

Walter used the move and reorganization to accomplish more of his goals as Director of the Belarus Service. The Service was enlarged, and he brought in younger journalists directly from Belarus. He also finalized setting up an official RFE/RL bureau in Minsk. The number of hours for broadcasting in Belarusian was increased, a greater variety of programs was added, and, eventually, internet programming was begun. Walter felt satisfaction in the increasing impact the Radios' programming was having on its audience in Belarus, particularly since the broadcasts were no longer being jammed.

At the same time, Walter participated in larger Radios activities, for instance, inaugurating and serving as Chairman of the Service Directors' Council.

I felt somewhat sad, as we moved the rest of our furnishings from our lovely Bogenhausen garden apartment in Munich to Prague, but then, I'd not been in Munich much recently. Walter was happy to be moving back to the Czech Republic – a Slavic country, near relatives, and where childhood memories were strong.

By the time we were leaving Munich, housing was becoming more accessible in Prague. We found a larger, airy apartment on the second floor of a modern home on Nad Zelivkou, a street in the section of Prague called Nebusice. The nearby International School also attracted interesting people to the area.

"Look at the beautiful Sarka park right across the street from our apartment!" I exclaimed, immediately relating to the forest of tall evergreens, reminiscent of my Pacific Northwest childhood environment. I was getting a fresh view of what life in Prague could be like. Optimism was replacing dreariness.

But that optimism was short-lived, as we began to encounter more of the realities of daily life in an early post-Communist country. We now personally faced issues I'd earlier questioned: How could a whole governing structure be totally changed: the laws and the authorities applying them? Also, it was obvious that individuals simply could not change overnight from the paranoia of constant fear to a more natural openness. Some predicted the task might take decades.

The challenges were many. "The wild, wild East" was the moniker given to the Eastern European countries emerging from Communism. Just as in our American Wild West, law and order were not always easily found. Although, later, we experienced the opportunities available in this evolving environment, in the beginning it was an unsettling atmosphere in which to live. We had to learn to navigate many pitfalls.

For example, we saw evidence of criminal street-corner negotiations after the Russian Mafia moved into Prague and began controlling drug, weapons, and prostitute trafficking; money laundering; and various other criminal activities. When walking downtown, I became much more cautious, after one of Walter's colleagues was murdered in an underpass I often used.

One day, I ordered a taxi to take me from our home to the Ruzyne airport, located just one town over. The driver placed my three matching bags into the trunk, as I said,

"Letiste" (airport). The driver reached the end of the street and turned right, instead of left, toward the airport. I said,

"Ne, ne (no)" and pointed the other way. I expected that he would turn around at the next corner. He just kept going toward the town of Suchdol and then turned toward the countryside.

Now I was getting really upset with him. I sat forward in the seat to see and write down his cab number. He saw what I was doing and understood that I intended to report him. His scowl was murderous. By now, we were on a smaller road in a thickly wooded area, without traffic. Suddenly, I recalled the story of a friend who'd ordered a taxi, then been robbed, beaten, and dumped in the woods by the taxi driver.

That vision made me berate myself, Okay, Joanne, this situation could turn deadly; I'd better calm down and pray my way out of this. I turned from my rising emotional panic and became very quiet. I lowered my head and prayerfully affirmed: God is ever-present, and He is directing the driver, me, and everyone – right at this moment, right in this cab. Only good can be the outcome.

Finally, the driver turned toward the airport, saying, "Sorry, not know way." Like heck, I thought, but I kept silent, still prayerfully supporting a good outcome. I wasn't going to stop praying until I was out of the taxi. Thankfully, it was still in time for my flight. I was grateful to be on my way safely and even more eager for a month of respite in America, away from the chaos of living in Eastern Europe.

Many similar experiences occurred in transit to and from the Czech Republic. Sometimes these events made me feel very unsettled and insecure. Often, I wanted to stay home, so as not to put myself at risk "out there." I leaned even more on my faith in God's ever-present protecting power to guide me away from, or get me out of, whatever difficult situations I might encounter.

In those early days, it was hard not to subscribe to the moniker of Prague as "The Wild, Wild East." It did, indeed, resemble the unbridled lawlessness of our Wild West.

Horomerice atrium house, under reconstruction

25
THE CORRUPTION EPIDEMIC

At one point, the local English-language weekly newspaper, the *Prague Post*, ran a headline: "Corruption Epidemic." We were soon to encounter this epidemic, as well as the incompetence bred by the Communist system.

One Saturday afternoon, during our walk in the Sarka woods, Walter came up with an idea:

"I've been thinking, since we may be staying in Prague for an extended time, we could be building equity, if we bought a house here. Cousin Petr thought we might be able to arrange it." By then, some homes had been returned to their previous owners, and a few new houses were being built.

I wasn't so sure about making our move seem that permanent. But Walter was convinced this was the direction we should take, and so I agreed to at least look. Consequently, we started a long and tedious period of house hunting. Few units were available, and many foreigners were looking.

One day, we made an appointment to see a partially-built house in the village of Horomerice, north of Prague. We almost didn't go in. The house looked like a closed up fortress on the outside, with small, high grilled windows peeking out of the stucco, two-feet-thick walls.

We stepped into the living room, and my breathing almost stopped, as my eyes traveled around the U-shaped contemporary home, with its many picture windows looking out onto a private atrium courtyard. It was just the type of home I'd always dreamed of.

I turned to Walter – even without seeing the rest of the house – and whispered, "This is it. Ask how much they want for it."

Walter was a little taken aback, wanting to be more cautious. But, within a few days, we'd agreed to buy the house. It was being built as a two-family house, one unit replicated above the other. The idea of added, continuing rental income appealed to Walter. And since it was still being built, we felt it would be an advantage to be able to choose the flooring and kitchen arrangement we wanted. I'd enjoyed designing a new kitchen in Mountain Lakes and looked forward to the challenge of doing so in Prague.

The term, "being built," however, was the key to great troubles that lay ahead.

Although Western-style real estate and zoning laws were not yet fully in place, we tried to protect ourselves in the contract by stating that we would pay in increments, with the last payment being given to the builder upon occupancy. We'd heard many stories of foreigners who'd lost all their money after giving in to the demand of a builder for the full amount up front. Local builders simply did not have start-up cash.

After signing the contract, we were quickly thrown into the graft and corruption convulsing this developing country. For instance, in our contract, we'd required a telephone before moving in. Later, the builders told us that they needed an extra $4,000 from us, as a required bribe to the local government official handling telephone connections – otherwise, it would be two to four years before we could get a telephone. We insisted to them that we had to have a telephone (it was before cell phones became available), but we also said we would not support corruption by giving bribe money. The builders' solution: arranging, for a smaller payment to a neighbor, to run a line from the neighbor's telephone to our house.

Also, we soon realized that the owners-builders (two cousins) were totally incompetent. After several months of watching the worsening construction situation, I yelled at Walter one evening,

"We have to *do* something! Everything those builders do is wrong. First, they couldn't figure out how to build stairs going to the second floor: it's ridiculous that *we* had to design a way to get up there. It's bad enough they don't use simple tools like a plumb line, so there's not even one straight wall, but yesterday I tripped on the uneven kitchen floor tiles they'd just installed. Between the flimsy interim gas tank lines, sagging ceilings, and water damage from pipes not properly connected, it just seems like we're going to have to redo everything. And they don't pay any attention to me. When I mention something that needs adjusting, they just smirk and walk off. I can't stand it anymore!" That finished my long harangue; I threw my hands up in the air, near hysteria.

"Now, Joanne, calm down. Yesterday I talked to Petr. He said there's not really much we can do. There isn't any use suing them, since they don't have much money. The builders own the property until we make the final payment, so we'd lose everything if we tried to go any other route than to continue with them."

It sounded so hopeless; I felt trapped in a disastrous situation. I started to sob uncontrollably. Walter came over and put his arms tightly around me until I settled into a whimper.

This sense of despair wasn't natural to me. Later that evening, I recalled a time in America when a colleague had approached me with a telling revelation: "Joanne, why is it that you smile all the time?" I thought it was strange that he would feel disconcerted by someone who smiles. "I didn't realize I did," I replied. "But I guess everyone has a choice whether to frown or smile. I choose to smile and feel happy." But I realized that I hadn't smiled very often lately – and that needed to change.

I chastised myself, Okay, Joanne, you may not be able to do anything about the incompetent builders, but you have to find a way to handle your own reactions and stop yourself from slipping into a depression.

There seemed to be three avenues to offset what was happening around me. One, of course, was to spend more time in Italy – except, during the summer, I didn't have an apartment there, so it meant living in the motor home.

Another distraction was shifting my focus from the house to creating a lovely Tuscan-like garden, with the help of a British garden designer. It was a wonderland of shapes and sizes and colors. Besides red and green vines covering the garden walls, I planted apple and quince trees and a butterfly bush. Red and yellow tulips and various shades of lilacs blossomed in the spring, red geraniums cascaded down the patio wall in summer, and yellow chrysanthemums carpeted the middle of the garden in the fall. From Italy, I brought a graceful Florentine bird bath and two spiked green cypresses. The garden was a place of beauty, and it helped to bring joy back into my life.

I also finished painting and decorating the back bedroom, making it a calm retreat, so that I could shut out some of the noise and distress created during the building completion. It became a haven to retire into for respite and prayer, and I prayed diligently to find an answer to the shoddy construction.

Interestingly, the answer came when the builders left the worksite, soon after our second-to-last payment. The whole upstairs apartment was left unfinished. By then, we'd moved into the house with a temporary occupancy permit. To finish the work, we hired a recommended contractor who'd been well trained in Germany. He also ended up having to redo much of the sloppy work.

Later, even with extensive documentation and testimony from professionals, a still-Communist judge (one obviously not sympathetic to "rich" Americans) awarded the builder the rest of the payment, as well as a penalty. It was a costly lesson, but at least, after several years, the house and the accompanying ordeal were finished. Walter's comment was, "It's just money; let's move on."

As a celebration of the house being finished, we invited several neighbors who'd been friendly to us for an American-style barbecue. Too late, the awkward silence and frowning glances made us realize that some of these neighbors had spied upon and informed on other neighbors, and it wasn't conducive to the friendly neighborhood event we'd hoped for.

A Thanksgiving dinner with our relatives was more successful, with some of them recalling, years later, the "American Holiday" together when we counted our blessings.

Life in early post-Communist Prague had not been easy, but there was one aspect for which I was grateful. Walter and I were working closely together again: planning, making decisions, and working through the house situation, as well as starting to build a new life together in Prague. The separateness I'd felt, when we lived in Munich, was past.

Czech President Vaclav Havel, at Dissidents Conference

26
A CIVIL SOCIETY DAWNS

After several years of experiencing the chaos and corruption of a floundering nation, while the Czech Republic slowly evolved from Communism to democracy, we began to see order and progress emerge.

I was fascinated by the political struggle that surrounded the question of *how* to bring the Czech Republic into the Western European framework. The *Prague Post* called it "The conflict of the two Vaclavs." Vaclav Klaus, the strong Prime Minister, held that economic progress, through the development of private enterprise, was the key to Westernizing. Whereas, the less political former playwright, President Vaclav Havel, felt that the most important factor was to rebuild what he called "A Civil Society." The differences seemed to epitomize the material improvements versus the moral renewal question of life and raised the issue: Which is more important, or should come first?

Czechs, themselves, were conflicted about the sudden changes in their lives. Many wanted the freedoms and economic advantages of the West, but some weren't aware of the civil responsibilities that usually accompanied those privileges. We found that younger Czechs were often more optimistic, while the older generation sometimes bemoaned the lack of disciplined organization previously experienced in Communist times. I wondered, How could they so soon forget the fear and deprivation of those times?

One day, several years after this renewal had started, Walter and I checked out the many aisles of the British-owned Tesco, the first large supermarket to open on the outskirts of Prague. As I was readying supper that night, I thought back to the steps toward the economic development this day represented, as we'd seen free enterprise spring up in one place, then another.

Most of the early investors came from foreign countries, eager to get a foothold in this developing market. First, a few small Belgian and Austrian grocery chains opened in the city, offering upgraded canned goods. Then, I absolutely drooled at the beautifully fresh fruits and vegetables in a new store, Fruits de France. No more wilted carrots, cabbages and potatoes for me!

"This is a real upgrade!" I'd pronounced, on hearing that K-mart had arrived in town, with its vast array of inexpensive, but well-made, merchandise. It even had smiling staff. Admittedly, K-mart did not make the same impression on me back in the States – it was only in comparison to the shoddy items and surly staff still found in the previously government-owned Czech stores.

I remembered the day when I called to Walter, in exasperation, "What are we going to do about this?" It was the third time we'd received a new sofa from IKEA, only to find that each new one was still lopsided. The reason? IKEA had switched its sofa manufacturing to a local factory.

I felt that things were changing for the better, but concluded that more intensive oversight and training, and probably additional investment in more modern equipment, was still needed in order for Czech standards to be raised to Western expectations.

Walter called to me from the patio, then, to say that the grill was ready. We'd gotten a good steak – a real treat in this country – from Tesco and were celebrating with an outdoor barbecue. Our lovely garden made it a special pleasure. We were surrounded by blooming red geraniums cascading down the patio wall and many different-colored butterflies hovering over the deep purple buddleia.

The next day, President Havel was quoted in the *Prague Post* about the need for a transcendent spiritual renewal in the citizens, to offset graft and corruption. Havel urged refurbished morals and improved personal ethics as essential to building a strong new nation. The newspaper noted that these chidings weren't always appreciated by all Czech citizens. That article made me think about the other side of that coin of renewal, building a "Civil Society". I wondered, What does that really mean?

I went to the bookshelf and took out an article that Havel had written, to better define his meaning. In it, he complained that the Communists had destroyed a sense of community and close relationships by their reign of fear, with informants being everywhere. Part of the term Civil Society, Havel said, meant rebuilding a sense of strong, supportive community, with people genuinely caring about each other. Perhaps this was harder to accomplish, I thought, than changing the laws to provide for private businesses to flourish.

Over the forty years of Communist rule, Havel's moral courage often landed him in jail, but this quality and experience also marked him as a major dissident figure who was not afraid to stand up for what was right. He was also a beacon for many other nations, as when he spoke on this theme to the Conference of Dissidents.

I thought about some of the various paths I'd seen used to build this new society. The newly elected democratic government sought assistance from Western sources, and many Westerners flooded into the Czech Republic, including some 30,000 Americans. Some of the Westerners were specialists in updating various laws. Others were Peace Corps-types, come to assist in building new organizations, such as the Czech Business Women's Organization. Still others were educators, come to help upgrade the nation's curriculum, which were previously geared to Communist values. Some returning émigrés brought together ordinary Czech citizens, as well as influential individuals, to expose them to new ideas. Of course, some Westerners mainly wanted to make large profits by getting their own interests and businesses in on the ground floor of a newly opened market.

Like most foreigners, I, too, was excited about being involved in this renewal of a nation, and participated in small ways. For instance, one afternoon, I was going to a High Tea at Jana's home. Jana was a tall, thin, dark-haired woman in her middle years, poised, and always fashionably dressed. She and her husband had left Prague in the aftermath of the 1968 Soviet crackdown of Dubcek's Prague Spring, the short-lived, softened form of Communism. They settled in Canada, but had recently returned. Her husband, Eduard, was a government official (and later, a Senator) in the Czech Republic.

These monthly High Teas, which included outstanding speakers, were one avenue she used to bring new ideas to many of her high-level contacts in the country. The programs included topics such as "Environmental Health Hazards of Living in Prague" and

"Volunteerism", which was a concept unfamiliar to most Czechs. The group also coordinated efforts of other organizations in the country, for example, in giving assistance after the Moravian floods. In the beginning, some of the gatherings were in English and some in Czech, with translators available. From the speakers, I learned much about Czechs and their struggle to rise out of their recent oppression.

My path to these more Czech-related activities had started by my joining the International Women's Club, whose meetings were in English. I enjoyed the monthly meetings with speakers, their trips around the Czech Republic, and the various interest groups, and I eventually contributed several programs to the group. Friends from the club were associated with the embassies, or with the many new organizations and businesses now operating in Prague. Here, there was no established hierarchy, as in Munich; we were all new and wanting to connect with others.

But I really wanted to meet and get to know more Czechs. At an International Women's Club meeting, I heard about the APM, the Business and Professional Women's Association of the Czech Republic; their early meetings were also in English. During my first meeting with the APM, I was introduced to the Peace Corps representative from the United States. She said she had been sent to Prague for a year, to help Czech women develop Western business skills.

When I later shared with the group my seminar, "Setting Life and Career Goals," there were varying responses, from: "These are totally new ideas!" and "It's really helpful to think about keeping a balance of goals in all areas of life," to grumblings heard on the side "How could writing affirmations make a difference in getting what you want?" Lives had been so governmentally regulated that to set one's own life course was a new and still uncomfortable idea.

It was at one of their meetings that I met Jana. I was happy to join the board of her group, the International Women's Network, and contribute to their programs, though my frequent travels to Italy sometimes interfered with my participation. However, I was glad to be here for today's High Tea.

After the other guests left, while I helped Jana put dishes back in the kitchen, she shared this insight:

"You know, Joanne, returning Czechs don't always have an easy time reintegrating."

"Is that because life is so different here, than in Canada?" I asked.

"No, it's more because of the attitude of the Czechs who remained," she answered, to my surprise. "There's a lot of envy and resentment from those who stayed here. They're not sure we have a right to suggest to them how to develop their country."

"That's too bad," I responded. "People like you can contribute so much Western know-how, and that's what's needed. Actually, I think you *do* impact much of the change going on here. I feel that your gatherings contribute a great deal to building the Civil Society Havel speaks about."

Dream Boards and soaring goals

27
SEEKING DEEPER MEANING

At first, it seemed to me that the emphasis of most Czechs was just to achieve a degree of the materialism of the West. Later, I also sensed a desire in many for a renewed spiritual aspect to life. For instance, Cousin Helena became interested in meditation-based Reiki.

"Why do you believe that?" was a probing question her daughter, Anna, asked me several times, as she appeared to be seeking a deeper meaning to life. (We were, by then, using more Western names for our relatives.) That was a question also asked repeatedly by our business associate, Ludmila, as she endeavored to understand Western thinking. I was heartened to recognize this searching about values, which I felt was an important building-block toward a Civil Society.

While our relatives and others in the Czech Republic were looking for meaning in a new life, I met with a group of people who had struggled to keep alive their own spark of spirituality: the Prague Christian Science Society, which had survived through the years of Communist atheism. Through church friends in the States, I'd heard how Bibles, other books, and literature had been smuggled in to the group, during those years.

Melanie was the member who seemed to have helped hold that Society together, when it was dangerous to be openly religious – especially, since she was affiliated with a church which was based in the United States. Melanie was a blonde bundle of energy, always positive and very devoted to the ministry of prayerful healing. I could imagine how her loving smile and ready laughter must have lightened the burdens of other members.

One day after church, Melanie and several of the group quietly shared with me some of their travails during Communist times:

"We would meet in different people's apartments whenever we could arrange it, coming in silently, one by one, hoping that the house informer wouldn't become aware," Melanie said.

"Most of us lost our jobs, or were given menial work, when our church attendance was discovered," another member added, with sad regret for those lost years.

After that exchange, I felt renewed gratitude for America's freedom of religion, a freedom that I'd taken so much for granted. I thought, What courage it had taken to hold on to faith in anti-religious Communist times!

There were many activities aimed at changing the dynamic of the country. Once, I attended a symposium in English at a university, entitled "Teaching Business Ethics." Several speakers brought out the need for developing critical thinking again, while teaching ethics to students. During the question period, I asked,

"Given that in the United States we use a Judeo-Christian basis for determining ethics, what will you be using here as a basis?"

In responding, every Czech expert on the panel seemed to agree, "We talk together and decide what is ethical." I wasn't convinced that this humanist basis for building a new ethos would be sufficient, given the rampant corruption seen in so many areas of life there.

We ourselves encountered a problem with ethics issues, in trying to build our Interdiam business in the Czech Republic. After we'd built a base of interested associates, the grand opening of the business was delayed several years. In the meantime, before the product lines were legally imported, the same goods were being smuggled into the country. Upon hearing about the smuggling, the typical response from our associates went something like this:

"Why can't you bring in these products, too? You have a motor home and could easily do it."

"Because it's illegal," I answered.

"But everyone is doing it," was the insistent reply.

It was disheartening to me. They couldn't seem to comprehend that we wouldn't do it just because it wasn't right. They were decent people, but had been brought up under a regime where trying to circumvent the government was considered proper, and often necessary, behavior. Our hope was that what they currently considered as being our "unreasonable" insistence on business integrity might later be looked on as a model to follow.

After the official opening, our business did start to grow, though it didn't flourish for us in the Czech Republic, as we had hoped. But, there was feedback that encouraged us to feel we had contributed something of value to the lives of our associates. For instance, one training activity was a Dream Board Session, where I asked associates to bring magazines related to things important to them. The exercise was to cut out and paste onto the poster board words or images representative of things they wanted in their lives, then to post the board where they'd see it daily, as a reminder to work toward those goals. This followed the dictum "Visualize it, in order to actualize it."

Many years later, Suzana, a Czech ex-pat who joined our Prague business in the mid-1990s, said,

"I still have that Dream Board. I was struck by the fact that probably 90% of my goals came true: living in Prague and New York, providing excellent schools for my girls, making a good living and doing charity work – even a van that my father picked up in New York to bring here. Without ever seeing my board, he bought exactly the car, including the color. I am a firm believer! Nicole, Katerina (her children), and I do these every few years now."

Vladimir was another Czech business associate who participated in the Dream Board Sessions. "Buy my apartment" was one phrase placed on his poster, as well as a number of items related to sailing, his favorite pastime. Eventually, he purchased his apartment and a sailboat, and his family spent many enjoyable hours sailing on the Vltava River.

Not all goals placed on the Dream Boards were for material items; some were for improving qualities of character or about relationships.

With the Radios' move to Prague in 1995, I also attended more activities at Radio Free Europe/Radio Liberty. The new RFE/RL headquarters was a centrally-located facility with large meeting halls, so important conferences and receptions were sometimes held there. As a spouse, I was allowed to attend, and I enjoyed the intellectual stimulation they afforded. At various meetings and receptions we spoke with key leaders, such as Czech President

Vaclav Havel, First Lady Hillary Clinton, and the then United
Nations Ambassador, Madeline Albright.

Toward the end of our experience in Prague, a new President of
the Radios arrived, Tom Dine. He and his wife, Joan, had previously
served in the Peace Corps. I found her very simpatico and interested
in communicating with the local community, and so I invited her to
several of the local organizations I was involved with.

Eventually, we worked together with Jana, of the International
Women's Network, to coordinate a program for Radios' personnel,
"The Status of Women in the Czech Republic." The goal was to
sensitize people at the Radios to the current role of women in Czech
society. Speakers at the event represented the Open Society Fund,
Foundation Our Child, and the Public Opinion Research Institute.
They were all organizations working to improve conditions in the
Czech Republic.

These were some of the points made in the meeting:

"Czech women," one speaker said, "are not interested in an
aggressive women's movement, like the Betty Friedan one in the
United States. Women here heard enough harping about equality
of men and women in the Communist era."

"On the other hand," someone else interjected, "business women
in the Czech Republic do not have equal opportunity for top jobs,
now. Many want to learn how to break through the so-called 'glass
ceiling'."

Another added, "With incomes rising substantially, now that we
have a freer market, there is a growing middle class. Many women
are grateful to have the option to stay home, raise their children,
and pursue their own interests. Before, it was our 'patriotic duty' to
work at whatever job we were assigned."

Some other problem areas were addressed: "The chaos of
changing times has put much stress onto families. As a society, we

need to be providing more services to women who are caught up in abusive home situations."

Many of the questions raised pinpointed serious problems, but they also seemed to encapsulate the humanizing Civil Society called for by President Havel.

By the end of the meeting, I felt encouraged about the progress in the Czech Republic, and thought, Times are indeed changing. Not only are the trappings of a free enterprise society emerging, but changes in thinking patterns are beginning to underpin the material gains.

A weary wanderer

28
WINDING DOWN

Retirement was in sight by the late 1990s. Walter and I were well into our 60s, and he was finishing ten years at the Radios. We'd been talking about staying for several more years in Europe, after Walter stopped working at the Radios. The plan was for us to get a bigger apartment in Italy, live there most of the year, secure our business there, and also take time to enjoy Italy together.

I felt we needed to start thinking about our return to the States, as well. That conversation started one night in our Czech village home:

"Walter, where were you thinking we might live when we go back to the States?"

"Well, maybe New York City?"

"Really? But the city is so dirty, and it's stressful living there." My life had seemed too stressful in Europe, with all the traveling back and forth. I wanted a quieter lifestyle.

"Yes, but you have the advantage of being right where everything is happening. And I don't want all that yard work again, like we had in Mountain Lakes."

"I can appreciate that," I said. "I just don't think I'd like that kind of hectic city life, at this point. Actually, I was thinking this might be a time when we could change areas entirely – maybe move nearer my family in the Pacific Northwest or to southern California, where we could swim every day." I'd yearned for a more casual, open Western atmosphere: the East Coast seemed too traditional for me.

"But the kids are in New Jersey," countered Walter.

"Who knows how long they'll be there. They might move. And have you forgotten? When we left New Jersey, I said I didn't want to ever go back to that heat and humidity again. It was really bothering me in the summers."

"Oh, it wasn't that bad. Anyway, I want to be near the Belarusian community."

"I understand that's important to you. But what about me: how about doing what I want, this time?" Even as I said it, rather petulantly, my conscience told me, Okay, so our main goal in coming to Europe was for Walter to work at the Radios, but I was glad to be coming to Europe too; it wasn't just for him.

This was obviously going to be a process: to work through our differences, in order to find the right location for our next, more permanent home in the States. It took over a year of going back and forth in thinking and discussions to arrive at a satisfying conclusion.

In the meantime, we each had to disengage ourselves from our European involvements and get mentally ready for the next move.

One event stands out in my mind, as a turning point for me. The motor home was being repaired, so I'd flown down to Rome from Prague for several special meetings in Tuscany.

At the end of the trip, I boarded the train in Florence, headed for the airport in Rome. It was summer, hot and humid, and I was exhausted from my whirlwind of work that week.

Since there'd been a nationwide train strike earlier in the week, I was grateful to be on a train for Rome, although I'd had to take the slower Local, instead of the Express. Looking around my train compartment, I noted how different the Local passengers were from my usual International Express crowd: rather than the matched luggage of those Express business types, the local travelers carried all sorts of bags tied with rope, with things sticking out, and there was the garlicky smell of homemade salami sandwiches hovering in the air.

As I leaned back in my seat, I pushed my thoughts ahead to the immediate future: I was really looking forward to the cool summer that Prague was having and to seeing Walter. I'd planned my return for Friday, so that we could have a relaxed weekend together.

By that time, I was getting drowsy, so I tucked my bag securely under my feet, wrapped my purse handle around my arm tightly, and lay back to snooze. I figured I'd be roused when everybody got up to leave at the end of the line in Rome.

I woke with a start. I looked at my watch and questioned, Shouldn't we be there already? "Where are we?" I asked the conductor . . . "What? This train goes to Naples?" No! "Conductor, can I get off at the next stop? I missed the Rome stop, and I have a plane to catch." . . . "You mean it was local to Rome, and now it's non-stop to Naples? Oh, my God!"

I had to struggle with my emotions. Joanne, just get hold of yourself; crying isn't going to help. Think! Can I get another train back in time for my flight? No, probably not. Okay, so if I call the airline before the plane leaves, maybe I can change my ticket for a fee – at least I won't lose the whole amount, then.

I continued berating myself. What a stupid thing to do! I'm going to have to get a hotel room – probably in Rome near the train station would be best. But it's going to cost a lot of extra money.

By then, the train had arrived in Naples. It's not a city I enjoy because of previous crime-related experiences, so I was nervously suspicious of every lounging stranger at the station. It was also the 2 p.m. siesta time, so the travel agency, which I needed in order to change my flight, was closed until 4. I had too much luggage to walk far, but at least there was a close-by café I could wait in and pray for everything to somehow work out.

And it did work out. I had enough lire left to pay for the train back to Rome, and the Naples travel agent was able to contact the Czech airline in time to change my flight, without extra payment.

In Rome, I found that the Best Western hotel near the train station had one last room. They woke me at 3 a.m. so that I could get the train to the airport in time for the 5:30 flight.

Upon arriving home, Walter – rather than giving me an earned reprimand – realized I'd been through quite an ordeal and just gave me a big hug and put me to bed. I slept for most of the next two days – definitely ruining my plans for a reunion weekend!

For a couple of days after this experience, I felt like a weary wanderer, tired of all these "exciting" experiences. But I realized that I needed to wipe that depressing feeling out of my thinking, so I started to recall all the just-fun things we'd done in Europe, as compared to the more politically-oriented or business activities. Those included purchasing thin batiste blouses at Lake Balaton in Hungary; hiking over fragrant fields of herbs to reach the beach on the Greek isle of Symi; covering ourselves with mud and jumping into the bubbling waters off the Sicilian isle of Volcano; and feasting on the many different preparations of snails in the French Provence region. So many fond memories flooded in; I knew our photo album would bring them all back, after we returned to America.

Walter was also winding down his Radio Free Europe/Radio Liberty activities.

"This has been such a rewarding time to serve at the Radios," Walter said, one evening as we snuggled on the sofa together, "with all the historic changes taking place in Eastern Europe! But now I feel it's time for the younger crowd to take over; they're more capable, anyway, with some of the new internet trends."

"Good," I replied, "it's time to let go of that grind of daily broadcasting. Now is the time to rent a bigger place in Italy, so we can enjoy several more years together in Europe." Thus, Walter retired from the Radios in late 1998, with the Directorship being assumed by Alexander, a computer-savvy young journalist from Belarus. Walter and I followed our plan for the next three years, with one short interlude, when he filled in again as Acting Director of the Belarus Service.

At Walter's retirement, on October 30, 1998, Tom Dine, then President of Radio Free Europe/Radio Liberty, broadcast these words about Walter:

"As the head of our broadcasts to dictatorial Belarus, Walter emerged as a significant figure in the history of Belarus and in the history of Radio Free Europe/Radio Liberty. He joined Radio Liberty as an analyst and then became the Director of the Belarus Service. It's in this position that he became an advocate of democracy, of an open society, of bringing the rule of law to Belarus. Walter became a change agent – and therefore an important person in history. I am happy to have worked with such a man."

Walter was still actively contributing to Belarusian progress, but more personally, rather than officially representing the Radios.

"Joanne, I'm off to Belarus on Friday," Walter called over to me from the study one day, soon after retiring from his job. "They've set up a number of seminars around Minsk for the 'I Can Live Better' program." This was an all-day seminar he'd developed, using ideas learned in our business, but applicable to everyday life. For so long, those under authoritarian Communist rule had felt helpless to plan their own lives. "I Can Live Better" was aimed at offsetting that sense of helplessness, by introducing Belarusians to Western-style techniques to set and achieve their own goals in life.

"That's great, hon. I really think your program is an important contribution. It not only helps individuals change their way of thinking, it can help point the country in a better direction."

"I don't know about that, but at least it's a start," he replied, in his usual modest way.

Walter traveled a number of times to Belarus, where he presented the seminars. He developed a support network and then trained others as teachers. Later, when political conditions worsened, it wasn't wise for Walter to travel there. Then, he arranged for videos of the program to be made, so that people could still view them in their own homes. A number of participants credited the program with changing their thinking substantially, so that, instead of just accepting or complaining about their situations, they felt they could begin to direct their own lives again.

(Unfortunately, this kind of thinking became untenable in Belarus during the 17-year regime of President Alexander Lukashenka, whom the Western press called "the last dictator in Europe." After Lukashenka's election in 1994, he dissolved the legitimate parliament, controlled the media, brutalized peaceful demonstrators, and imprisoned opposition leaders. Many of

Walter's contacts in Belarus either fled to asylum in the West, or became one of the "disappeared.")

I was relieved that Walter was no longer travelling into the deteriorating situation in Belarus, though regretful for the Belarusians. However, I was looking forward to now being able to focus wholeheartedly on our next steps in life.

View from new home in Monmouth Beach, New Jersey

29
WHERE IS HOME?

Walter and I had gone back and forth in discussions about where to live in the States. For a long time, I'd been adamant about not wanting to live on the East Coast. Then I took a crucial trip, by myself, back to my family's farm in the Pacific Northwest. While there, it struck me: I don't really fit in the West, anymore. I'd miss the international activities we can participate in around New York and Washington, D.C.

I wondered, But where do I fit in best? I hadn't felt attuned to the more conservative, status quo thinking that I'd found on the East Coast: I like to try new ideas. I didn't want to live in a hectic city, but the suburbs sometimes seemed sterile. With my recent experiences in Europe coloring my thinking, I wasn't sure I could totally fit anywhere.

So, I looked at the question from a different angle: What do I want to do, when we move back to the States? I knew I didn't want to continue the same intense work schedule. I wanted quieter time to think about larger issues from a spiritual standpoint and to write. I wanted to be involved in church, interfaith, and community activities. After thinking this through, I realized I could do most of those things where Walter could also be close to Belarusian activity. And I did want to reconnect with our boys, though I still couldn't see myself living in New Jersey's summer heat and humidity. But maybe there's a compromise, I concluded. On that trip back to the States I'd made a decision, and I shared it with Walter, when I returned to Prague:

"How about finding a condo at the Jersey Shore, Walter? They say it's a lot cooler in the summer, with the sea breezes, and usually more temperate in the winter, than inland. I've always wanted to live on the ocean."

"That sounds like an interesting idea to explore," he replied.

I'd been praying a lot about what could provide us with a right sense of home. Early in married life, in December of 1960, we'd had an experience that redefined the word for me. We'd been married just three months, purchased all new walnut furniture, to my contemporary taste, and had just finished painting the last room in our 7th Ave. Brooklyn apartment. "A perfect home," I declared that night.

At about noon the next day, part of an airliner involved in a collision over Staten Island fell on our building, causing one wall to catch fire and the whole building to sway – almost collapsing like the brownstone next to it did. Fleeing the fiery chaos in our apartment, I ran into the snowstorm in my nightgown and bare feet. Then, I sought shelter in the nearby Christian Science Reading Room. Thinking that probably all our belongings were lost, I opened, at random, the book *Science and Health*, looking for comfort. The phrase that caught my attention was a definition of substance that read, in part, "Substance is that which is eternal and incapable of discord and decay" (page 468). It struck me: Yes, enduring substance is spiritual qualities, not material things.

Right then, my concept of home changed. I decided it was, in essence, the qualities of hospitality, loving kindness, and beautiful thoughts that we carry with us into whatever location we might call home. This idea helped me establish a more expansive sense of home during the more than 20 moves after that.

I'd heard people say, "Home is where your spices are." But my spices were spread among several locations. I realized that for me, at that point, home was synonymous with where Walter was. His presence was what completed my sense of home. That was where I felt comforted and comfortable.

In fact, I felt that the best serendipity of Walter's retirement was that I could get hugs in the middle of the day. If I'd been working on something intently and needed a break, or if something was troubling me, I'd get up and walk over to where Walter was sitting, put my arms around his neck, and say, "I need a hug". He'd look up with a solicitous smile and a warm gleam in his eyes and give me a strong hug, until I was sated. Then I could go back to work more relaxed, feeling loved and cared for. I knew that expression of home could be experienced anywhere. So now, I thought, we just need to find the right house in America, where we can best experience our sense of home.

On our summer trip back to New Jersey that year, we scouted out a number of communities, from Sandy Hook to Point Pleasant. We liked Monmouth Beach because it was a year-round community, not just a summer crowd. The area also had a direct bus and rail line into New York City, where many of Walter's Belarusian activities were located. We decided a townhouse would meet Walter's need for less yard work, so we left our specific preferences with two realtors and asked them to call us in Europe.

Almost a year later, we received a call from one of the realtors, who said she thought she had a good condo unit for us. One day later, I was on my way to the States for three days. I had appointments in Italy the next week, so I hoped that everything would work together to secure our next home in that short time.

The chance for the first unit fell through after a two-day bidding war. I stopped bidding when the price went 15% above the asking price. With one day left, I said, Okay, God, it's up to you. I've done all I can. The other realtor knew I was in town, but not where I was staying. She, too, had a possible unit, and so she called several motels, until she found me.

The unit she showed me was a large one-bedroom condo in the complex we wanted, and it had a magnificent view from the deck out over the Shrewsbury River estuary. My viewing of the unit was at dusk, and the shifting colors of the red, orange, and yellow sunset momentarily overwhelmed me. Then I spied a stalking egret standing regally still, as it waited for a fish to pass by, before suddenly darting its long neck toward the water. And I heard the cacophony of dozens of terns on a far island. I saw an osprey swoop down toward its pole nest, with dinner for the lone baby. Walter and I both appreciate the beauty of nature, and I was certain that we would never regret purchasing that townhome.

I was able to sign the contract one hour before I had to leave for the airport. On the plane, I gratefully kept thinking, Thank you, God! It just seemed so extraordinary that buying the house was, essentially, accomplished in one day.

Another part of getting ready for our eventual move to the States was putting our house in Prague up for sale. By that time, there were a goodly number of newer units on the market to choose from, and many in new developments, rather than in the middle of a small village. When our house wasn't getting much buyer attention, I began to pray that the right buyer would be aware of it and drawn to it. During my prayers, the word "utility" kept coming to mind, though it seemed a strange idea to describe the situation.

And what utility the house was to provide! The mayor of our village, Horomerice, decided it would be a perfect relocation spot for the village's post office downstairs and its library upstairs. The workers were delighted with the idea of increased space, in a newer building.

The sale wasn't completed until our final move back to the States, but still, we felt we could relax and enjoy several more years together in Tuscany.

Enjoying Italy together in Pisa and the Alps

30
SAVORING OUR LAST YEARS IN EUROPE

For three years after Walter's retirement we rented an apartment on the Mediterranean, in Tuscany, from October through April. We were still spending some time in Prague and our summers in the newly purchased condo on the Jersey shore – which made our lives somewhat fractured, but at least we were enjoying our different environments together.

By the late 1990s, life in Prague was vibrating with chic new shops, and many of our Czech friends were enjoying prosperous lifestyles. It was encouraging to watch our Czech relatives, over several years, buying their own homes, going on vacations to far-off places, and prospering in their professions or businesses. Their families also increased, with Katerina being added to Anna and

Peter's family; Mira and Sarka married and added three more children: Helena, Stepanka, and Suzana.

Our own time spent in Prague was now quite satisfying. I remember one week when we savored a bit of the good life available. It was Christmas, a great time to visit Prague. I shopped for gifts at the many stalls set up in the ancient town square and passed by the famous Czech puppets to purchase crystal beads and vases. Then, I found a stall that sold tapes of my favorite Czech rock group: the Yo-Yo Band; I thought the kids would enjoy them. On the way home from Christmas shopping, I stopped for awhile outside of Reduta, to sway to their soft-flowing music. Reduta was the jazz club where President Clinton endeared himself to the Czechs by jamming on the saxophone with a local band, during an evening off from a high-level conference in Prague.

There were so many different kinds of restaurants to choose from now. We ate one night at the Cedars Lebanese restaurant in Dejvice and another time at a restaurant that served wild game – a rarity in the States. Another evening, we drove to the east side of town for an English-language movie.

"Walter, let's check if the *Obecni Dum* (historic municipal house) still has those old-fashioned dances in the basement," I suggested on Saturday. They did indeed, and we tangoed and waltzed all evening.

After our church service on Sunday, we stopped at a historic church to listen to a concert of one of the famous Czech composers. (I forget whether it was Dvorak, Smetana, or Janacek.) Music was definitely an important aspect of life to Czechs; it was part of their diverse Slavic, mixed with Austro-Hungarian, cultural heritage. The nearby internet café was open, so we also stopped there to check our e-mail, before returning to our now-comfortable Horomerice home.

These more enjoyable activities in Prague were beginning to replace the negative memories of the house-building experience.

In Italy, our new apartment was a well-furnished two bedroom, three-balconied condo in Tirrenia, between the towns of Pisa and Livorno. It was just one block from the Mediterranean Sea, so the air was always fresh. Huge red geraniums flowed from planters on the balconies. I loved to sit and read on the larger balcony, and I appreciated that a tall pine tree provided privacy from neighbors. We moved many of our personal furnishings to this apartment, to make it feel like our main home.

The small town of Tirrenia was quiet and serene, compared to the bustling city of Florence, where I'd lived most of the time in Italy. Because Tirrenia was a summer resort town, there were many good restaurants, offering great grilled seafood and a variety of pastas. We also ate at favorite restaurants in the Tuscan hills: La Duna Verde in San Quirico or Lo Scorpione in Tavarnelle. I liked their pungent local wild boar and delicately truffled dishes.

At one point, I ran out of my best extra virgin olive oil, so we visited a small family-owned olive grove in the countryside. One of the secrets to producing delicious olive oil, they explained, was to pick the olives by hand, instead of shaking them onto the ground and bruising them.

Simple tasks, like daily shopping, became a pleasure. The seafood market, around the corner from the apartment, featured fish right off the boats in Livorno, with some fish still wiggling. As I entered the green grocer shop one morning, the owner greeted me with a hearty "Buon giorno!" And then he broke into an aria, just to celebrate the joy of life.

Walter and I started an almost daily routine: we walked, hand-in-hand, down to the beach, and smelled the fragrant roses that bloomed along the town's center street dividers. Then we put a blanket down on the sand and basked in the sun's warmth. It was a more relaxed life together than we'd had in many years.

It was also a time when more friends and relatives visited us from America. One day, I called to Walter,

"Hey, let's take Bill and Felicia (Walter's brother and his wife, who were visiting) on a day trip out to Cinque Terre. They love the outdoors." It was one of our favorite hiking tours: a visit to five ancient fishing villages, perched high above the Mediterranean, which only recently had a road built to them. Bill and Felicia greatly enjoyed the spectacular views of the jagged coastline. I especially remember the restaurant we ate at that afternoon: it had seats perched on the edge of a cliff. The steep drop-off view, right next to the foot of my chair, made me almost too dizzy to eat.

(Bill and Felicia's children represent the wanderlust of some Stankievich families: Paul and his wife now live in Mexico, George is in China, with only Andrew still in the United States. Walter's brother George lives in Prague, and George's daughter, Jana, is in California. Thus, we haven't had any large Stankievich family reunions, as I do with my farm family.)

As our third year together in Italy began, we revisited all the places and things that made us love Tuscany. We were etching them in our hearts and memories. In the springtime, when the fragrant yellow mimosa covered the hillsides, looking like fields of gold, we drove around the touristy Tuscan towns of Volterra – picking up a couple of alabaster plates for future gifts – and then on to San Gimignano and the larger Siena, known to so many tourists for its Palio horse races and flag-throwing parade around the square. One of the disadvantages of visiting these ancient cities, however, was that we sometimes had to pull in the side mirrors on our motor home, in order to navigate the narrow streets.

That whole area, from Cinque Terre over to Siena, seemed like our home territory. I was beginning to feel a strong tug between the thought of leaving my much loved Tuscany and the desire to live again in familiar, English-speaking America.

Of course, some of the memories in Italy were more dramatic than idyllic. We'd worn out our first motor home, so when I went back to close on our U.S. condo, I also bought a new Pleasureway motor home and had it shipped to Europe. Because we kept the USA license plates, and this motor home was sleeker than European models, it generated unwanted attention several times.

The Camp Darby U.S. Army base was on the outskirts of Tirrenia, and we had limited recreational privileges there. Sometimes, for a change, we'd go there to get a taste of a Burger King American-style meal, or for a movie, and I also attended their Women's Club. But living near the American base did, at times, bring anti-Americanism close to home. One such instance was especially memorable.

One evening, I had a disconcerting intuition that something was amiss. I prayed to discern what, specifically, I needed to do, and a thought came that I shared with Walter,

"Walter, I don't know why, but I feel strongly that we need to park the motor home in our gated yard this weekend."

"You know the agreement with the owner was that we wouldn't do that," he replied. "Remember, one of the residents complained that the motor home had made it difficult for him to drive out of his parking space."

"I know, but there are very few other cars this weekend. And I just feel that we *have* to bring it inside. We're not going to be living here much longer anyway, even if they do complain."

He wasn't agreeing, but I went out, unlocked the gate, and drove the motor home inside, parking it as far out of the way as I could.

The next Monday I was at the Army base, when a friend called over to me,

"Hi, Joanne. Hey, were you guys hit over the weekend? You live in town, right?" she asked.

"Everything was fine. Why?"

"Didn't you hear? Over the weekend, American cars parked off-base were fire–bombed by those anarchists who've been demonstrating against our bombing in Serbia." Now, I put a different interpretation to the fire-cracker-type noises we'd heard over the weekend. And I understood why Army personnel were issued Italian license plates to flip down over their USA plates.

Our sleek motor home was very noticeable, especially with its USA license plates. It definitely would have been targeted, if it'd been on the street. And between the large gas tank and the propane bottle, any firebombing of that motor home would probably have taken out a good portion of our neighborhood, including us in our condo.

I sighed with relief, Sometimes it pays to go with intuition, regardless of the rules.

Business colleagues at Innsbruck convention

31
COUNTING THE REWARDS

Walter and I were still involved in our Italian business, though now acting in more of a counseling capacity. Local leadership had taken on more responsibilities, and we were preparing them for our departure.

One evening in our Tirrenia apartment, I reflected back on those years of building up the business in Italy. I recalled once giving a speech to a large group of business associates. As I sat down and looked over the crowd, I thought about what different individuals had contributed to the success of the business and how the close association with such a diverse group of people had enriched my life.

Interestingly, most of the people who came to mind were related to recognized leaders I'd started in the first year of working in

Florence. For instance, Dianne and the Swiss associate, Margot, who had helped train two current leaders, Elisa C. and Inga.

I looked out over the group that evening and found the smiling, motherly face of Elisa C., who was sitting with Louisa and Duccio, and with a number of her associates close by, like a supportive family. I recalled the proud joy on her face when Elisa showed me her name in a magazine, as a major contributor to the *Scuola Trinitaria* (school) in Andriamena, Madagascar. For many years she'd contributed much of her business income to support the building of that school.

Then I looked toward the back of the room where German-born Inga stood, with Francesco and some of the young Italian men he'd introduced to the business. Inga sometimes didn't have a full-time job, and she generously offered her time when I needed a translator, as, for instance, with high-energy Anna, a schoolteacher from Rome who wore me out with her fast-paced Italian and excited gesturing. Inga also sometimes offered me a room in her apartment in the summer, and she was a welcome companion for movie-going or a good meal together.

Sitting nearby was a retired couple, Erminia and Enrico, whom Inga had trained. After they heard of the need for children to get immunity-generating time away from the radiation-contaminated Chernobyl area, they brought children from Belarus into their sunny Florence home during the summers. This expression of generosity of spirit toward those in need encouraged us to open our hearts more, and we increased our support for Belarusian Chernobyl victims.

As I sat thinking about dramatic changes I'd seen in associates over the years, Inga's English friend, Jessica, came to mind. Jessica wasn't at the meeting, but I recalled when I'd first interviewed her on the Isle of Elba. She was so self-conscious that she couldn't look at me. Yet it was evident that she wanted to change. Persistently, through several self-development courses, her wry, self-deprecating humor changed to self-confidence. Through sales experience, she learned to assert herself with an alcoholic husband, get a divorce, and become a happy, independent person.

Next, our successful associate, Dianne, rose to speak at the meeting. She had interviewed and started many of the business associates there. Dianne was unwavering in teaching proven methods for developing a large business base, enabling others to progress. Some of those clapping the loudest for her were a group of former students who had started out just wanting some extra income while going to school. We'd watched them mature into fine young people, and many had built large businesses and achieved worthy personal goals.

For instance, when Stefania first started in the business with Dianne, her son was just a cute youngster who spent time drawing in the corner. Now, he was her reliable business partner. Nearby, was one of Stefania's associates, the very goal-oriented Laura M., a flutist student whose dream was to open a music school in Florence. She now had a burgeoning group of eager young associates with her. (We later applauded her graduation and then the opening of her successful music school.) Her focus was always to help others achieve their own potential.

Ioana was a chic Romanian student who had been studying for her Doctorate in Florence. Her bright enthusiasm inspired others, and she was here at the meeting with her fiancé, Raffaelle, a young man of old Florentine stock. (After their marriage, they presented us with a gift of hand-picked olive oil from their groves, high in the hills of Fiesole.)

I waved to fashionable Elisa P., who had just come in with others from Bologna; they had braved the Apennine mountain trip to attend this meeting. Part of Elisa's daytime job was arranging Italian settings for movie companies. She enjoyed the image consulting aspect of the business so much that she took a flight to California to train with my own teacher in that field, Bernice Kentner, author of *Color Me a Season*. Recently, she'd proudly shown me the Italian fashion magazine which featured a story she'd written about color analysis. It was gratifying to see someone not only take on, but improve, business ideas I'd presented.

Her associates from Bologna, including Laura P., illustrated another example of great personal growth. Laura had seemed very modest and unsure of her abilities in the beginning. I felt so proud of how she'd gradually taken on responsibility, and her leadership talents had matured immensely. The gentle graciousness expressed in that group also encouraged me to develop more gentleness in myself.

There had, indeed, been a mutual benefit from my work in Italy. Constant interchanges with the warmth and expressiveness of Italians had deeply changed me. For instance, I could see how my initial stiffness had softened: I hugged and touched others more freely now.

I was grateful for my business experiences. They had given me the opportunity to use and expand my talents in worthwhile ways. Certainly the blank slate I felt I'd arrived with in Munich had been filled to the full.

In the spring of 2001, after 13 years away, Walter and I closed the door on our European experiences and headed back to America.

On the plane, I thought back to how different world conditions were when we first came to Europe in 1988. The Iron Curtain still seemed so impenetrable then. The fear of informers and Secret Police ruled people's lives. Yet in ten short years, power had shifted. The Cold War era had given way to a new reality of freedom for Eastern Europe. Prospects now looked good for the Eastern European countries, guided by the possibility of joining the European Union; though, admittedly, for most of the former Soviet Republics, including Belarus, the future wasn't as clear. I was heartened with the courage and inventiveness of individual Czechs, Belarusians, and others, who were still struggling with these new realities in the quest for a better life. Both countries and people were redefining themselves.

Walter and I had also redefined ourselves during those years. Walter had left his engineer image behind. He felt satisfied that his work at the Radios and in Belarusian Diaspora activities had contributed to some of the historic changes. I could see that he was much more confident and self-assured than when we arrived in Europe; and his leadership skills had been well-honed. I knew that he would continue his efforts to help Belarusians when we arrived back in America.

We both felt happy to have connected with more of Walter's relatives. And I was grateful for the insights I'd gained about him, from seeing his childhood environments and having him share more of his family history. We'd definitely grown closer through our European experiences together.

Over the years, I'd been redefined, not just as the wife of the Director of the Belarus Service for Radio Free Europe/Radio Liberty, or an American enjoying tourist attractions in Europe, but as a successful businesswoman and a participant in the international communities in Florence and Prague.

For me, a deeper appreciation for culture and a historical perspective underpinning current events had been added to my thinking, which was now more from an international, rather than just American, perspective. I had also been exposed to and become more tolerant of diverse views and mores. I looked forward to whatever lay ahead, back in the United States, and wondered how our European experience might impact that life.

Working through some of our challenges had also increased my trust in God's ever-present help, and I was looking forward to participating in more church and inter-faith activities. I recognized that a change in my goals had occurred, exemplified in affirmations shifting from "Our business is successful" to "My purpose is to bring a loving and healing touch to all within my ken." My wanderlust had been sated.

I laughed, as I thought about a comment I'd recently made, "If I could have the courtyard home we built in Prague in the Tuscan hills, with German orderliness, and everyone speaking English around me, it would be the perfect setting in which to live life to the fullest." I realized that I'd had a taste of each of those lives, with the added spice of a scent of danger thrown in and a supportive life-companion. That little Pacific Northwest farm girl with big dreams couldn't have asked for more.

DISCUSSION GUIDE FOR BOOK CLUBS

1. Did the book give you a better understanding of the Cold War era and of the struggles of individuals and countries to adjust in the early post-Communist era? What specific events stand out in your mind?

2. How would you describe the relationship between Joanne and Walter and also their relationship with their children? If it differs from relationships in your family, please explain.

3. As Walter and Joanne evolved personally during their stay in Europe, do you recall what factors seemed to shape them, initially? What events or activities appeared pivotal in changing them?

4. Which of their more dangerous experiences is remembered most vividly? Why?

5. If you are familiar with any of the locations mentioned in the book, what are your most distinct memories there?

6. How would you characterize the coping skills of each of the main characters? If you have lived in a foreign country, compare your ways of coping with an unfamiliar language and culture with theirs.

You may wish to share one of your coping experiences on the author's website: www.JoanneIvyStankievich.com

ACKNOWLEDGMENTS

The events related in this book are based on daily notes recorded during the years covered, as well as from memory. The book is written from the author's perspective; therefore some memories may vary from those of the participants who are mentioned within the text. The dialog recreates the essence of conversations remembered and noted at the time. Perhaps any work which includes reproduced dialog should be called creative nonfiction. However, the events and dialog were carefully reviewed for accuracy by my husband, Walter, who was either present, or aware of most of the events, at the time they occurred. In a couple of scenes, as in the farm family reunion, several different events were condensed into one scene. However, the accuracy of the information was kept intact.

Accuracy of historical background, dates, and events were confirmed online and from books, including:

Cold War Radio, The Dangerous History of American Broadcasting in Europe, 1950-1989, by Richard H. Cummings
Communism, its Rise and Fall in the 20th Century, The Christian Science Monitor, edited by Richard E. Ralston
Dispatches from the Barricades, by John Simpson
Disturbing the Peace, by Vaclav Havel
Radio Free Europe and Radio Liberty, the CIA Years and Beyond, by A. Ross Johnson
The Cold War, a New History, by John Lewis Gaddis
The Europeans, by Luigi Barzini

My husband, Walter, was the one who suggested I write a book, and he encouraged me along the way – showing great patience when I was too busy to do mundane things, like making dinner.

235

He has been an invaluable assistant, giving me moral support, as well as help with editing and fact-checking. Our creative younger son, Steve, provided initial encouragement about my writing skills, saying, "This is great, Mom" when I sent him samples of my first writing endeavors. He also contributed by designing business cards and a website, and he assisted in photo preparation and book formatting. Thankfully, our older son, John, who works from home, was available during the day to offer practical guidance when I had computer glitches – once saving a large portion of the book from disappearing into oblivion.

Permission was granted for the use of the RFE/RL symbol used in the chapter 4 photo. Most of the other photos were taken with a family camera, with the exception of the chapter 11 dancers, provided by Alla Romano; and the chapter 27 dream board photo, provided by Suzana Potenec. I'm grateful for the back cover author photo, taken by Nancy Crabbe.

Evaluations of the manuscript changed my direction several times, thanks to Maribeth Pelly, my Marketing Coach; Steven Froias, editor of the TriCity News; and Marie Galastro, of MLG & Associates, my structural editor, who also did a yeoman's job as my copy editor. The book cover illustration was created by Arant Creative Group, and the cover design by MLG & Associates. Scott Asalone, of Asbury Park's Great Insights Press, was supportive and a conduit to others. My Administrative Assistant, Cookie Perry, has contributed substantially in gathering together promotional sources and material. Thanks go to Outskirts Press personnel, whose patient assistance helped me to navigate through the myriad of publishing decisions.

I am appreciative of all those who participated in writing workshops with me, offering insightful suggestions for various chapters as I honed my writing skills, shifting from a journalistic style to that of a memoir writer. Special thanks go to Loriann Fell, who taught my Memoir course at Rutgers University, spearheaded several subsequent writers' workshops, and helped with the proofreading of the book. Attendance at a Gotham writing workshop and at several Book Expo of America (BEA) conferences also supported my path. Many books on memoir writing and publishing have guided me, including *The Writer* magazine.

Some friends – from Germany, Italy, Czech Republic, and the USA – helped with, or read and gave input to, parts of the book in which they had participated, or about which they were experts, including Dianne Carriker, Bettie Dean, Russ and Rhonda Dean, Kathy Gardner, Inga Haeckl, Jewell Hood, Mirek Krist, Alexander Lukashuk, Jana Outratova, Wendy Romano, George Stankevich, Jan Zaprudnik, and Martins Zvaners.

I'm grateful, too, for friends and relatives around the world who have given encouragement to me, supported my efforts, and waited patiently as I've rewritten and restructured the book numerous times.

Some of the books and authors mentioned in this text:

Authors: John le Carre and Robert Ludlum
Bible references are from *The King James Bible*
Color Me a Season, by Bernice Kentner
Emerson's Essays, by Ralph Waldo Emerson
Release your Brakes, by James W. Newman
Science and Health with Key to the Scriptures, by Mary Baker Eddy
Sound of Thunder, by Ray Bradbury
The Power of Positive Thinking, by Norman Vincent Peale

The proceeds of this book and all its ancillary product proceeds will accrue to the tax exempt Monroe-Vilnia Foundation. This

238

foundation disseminates information about Belarus in the West, and promotes ideas related to democracy and individual liberties.

I hope that you will visit my website, www.JoanneIvyStankievich. com, for additional stories, planned events, travel photos and information, updates on the current Belarusian and Eastern European situations, and inspirational ideas.

COLD WAR TIMELINE

(Referred to in this book)

<u>February, 1945</u> Yalta Conference with Stalin, Churchill, and Roosevelt. Decisions made in the Yalta Agreement created "spheres of influence," which essentially divided Europe into an East-West scenario; the Cold War and arms race ensued.

<u>1949</u> NATO was formed (with the countering Warsaw Pact, under Soviet control, started in 1955).

<u>October – November 1956</u> An indigenous Hungarian Revolution, calling for more freedoms, was squelched by the invasion of massive Soviet and Warsaw pact troops.

<u>August, 1961</u> The Soviets erected the Berlin Wall around West Berlin, stopping the flow of East Berliners into West Berlin.

<u>January – August 1968</u> President Alexander Dubcek's Prague Spring brought liberalization to Czechoslovakia, until Soviet-led Warsaw Pact troops invaded and reinstated stronger Communist control.

<u>March, 1985</u> Mikhail Gorbachev became the Secretary General of the Communist Party in the USSR, encouraging the liberal policies of Glasnost (openness) and Perestroika (restructuring political and economic systems).

<u>Summer, 1989</u> The 1980s Solidarity Union Movement became a political force, calling for democratic elections in Poland, which they won in August, 1989.

<u>August, 1989</u> Cracks in the Iron Curtain widened when 13,000 East German tourists began a journey through newly fenceless Hungarian borders into Austria, then back up to West Germany.

<u>October 9, 1989</u> 70,000 East Germans marched in Leipzig with lighted candles, seeking greater freedoms; this started a similar, unstoppable movement all over the country.

<u>November, 1989</u> The new, still-Communist East German government opened borders to the West; the Berlin Wall was breached; talks began for democratic elections in East Germany.

<u>November, 1989</u> Czechoslovakia's Velvet Revolution began, as violence at student demonstrations sparked millions of dissenters to demand reforms.

<u>December, 1989</u> Playwright Vaclav Havel became President of Czechoslovakia, with Alexander Dubcek returning as Speaker of the Parliament.

<u>October 3, 1990</u> East and West Germany were reunited.

<u>1990 – early 1991</u> Most East European countries gained independence from Soviet control, including the Baltic Soviet Republics of Estonia, Latvia, and Lithuania.

<u>August 19 – 21, 1991</u> Hard-line Communists attempted a coup against Gorbachev to reverse Glasnost and Perestroika policies. But it was stopped by Boris Yeltsin and people yearning for greater freedoms.

<u>August 25, 1991</u> The Byelorussian Soviet Socialist Republic declared independence from Soviet control as the Republic of Belarus.

<u>December, 1991</u> The formation of the Commonwealth of Independent States (CIS), with Ukraine, Belarus, and Russia, essentially tolled the end of the Soviet Union.

<u>January, 1993</u> Czechoslovakia split into two countries: Czech Republic and Slovakia.

LIST OF ILLUSTRATIONS

European Map:

Displaying previous Iron Curtain and major cities mentioned in the book   xiv

Chapter photo captions:

244

CPSIA information can be obtained
at www.ICGtesting.com
Printed in the USA
FFOW03n1513240214
3810FF